A Friendly Guide to THE NEW TESTAMENT

FRANCIS J MOLONEY SDB

Contents

Published by
Garratt Publishing
32 Glenvale Crescent
Mulgrave, Vic. 3170
www.garrattpublishing.com.au

Copyright ©2010 Francis J Moloney

All rights reserved. Except as provided by the Australian copyright law, no part of this book may be reproduced in any way without permission in writing from the publisher.

Design and typesetting by Lynne Muir
Text editing by Ann M Philpott

Scripture quotations are drawn from the *New Revised Standard Version of the Bible*, copyright ©1989 by the Division of Christian Education of the National Council of the Churches of Christ in the USA. Used by permission. All rights reserved.

The icons reproduced on pages 1, 25, 28, 31, 34, 36, 39, 41 42, 46, 48 and 49 are the property of the Ukrainian Catholic Eparchy and are in the Ukrainian Catholic Cathedral of Ss Peter and Paul, North Melbourne. Credits for other images appear beside each image.

National Library of Australia
Cataloguing-in-Publication entry
  Moloney, Francis J.
  A friendly guide to the New Testament / Francis J Moloney.
  ISBN: 9781920721947 (pbk.)
  Series: Friendly guides.
  Subjects: Bible, N.T.—Criticism, interpretation, etc.
  225

Nihil Obstat: Reverend Gerard Diamond MA (Oxon), LSS, D Theol
Diocesan Censor
Imprimatur: Most Reverend Les Tomlinson DD Titular Bishop of Siniti, Vicar General
Date: 26th March 2010

The Nihil Obstat and Imprimatur are official declarations that a book or pamphlet is free of doctrinal or moral error. No implication is contained therein that those who have granted the Nihil Obstat and Imprimatur agree with the contents, opinions or statements expressed. They do not necessarily signify that the work is approved as a basic text for catechetical instruction.

FOREWORD 3

INTRODUCTION 4

UNDERSTANDING BIBLE REFERENCES 5

THE WORLD OF THE NEW TESTAMENT 6

　Judaism 6

　The Greco-Roman world 8

HOW DID THE NEW TESTAMENT COME INTO EXISTENCE? 10

　First things first 10

　Teaching before stories – Saint Paul 12

　The stories – the Gospels 14

　Pauline writings in the New Testament 16

　　1 and 2 Thessalonians 16
　　Colossians and Ephesians 16
　　The Pastoral Epistles 18
　　Paul's authentic letters 18
　　Letter to the Hebrews 19

　The remaining New Testament documents 20

　　The Catholic Epistles 20
　　Revelation 20

　The New Testament emerges 22

JESUS OF NAZARETH – A BIOGRAPHY 25

THE GOSPELS 28

　The synoptic Gospels 29

　Jesus as the pre-existent Logos 29

THE GOSPEL OF MARK 31

　The centrepiece of Mark's Gospel (Mark 8:22–9:7) 34

THE GOSPEL OF MATTHEW 36

　The universal mission of the Disciples (Matthew 28:16–20) 39

THE GOSPEL OF LUKE 41

　The parable of limitless compassion (Luke 15:1–32) 44

　The birth stories in Matthew 1–2 and Luke 1–2 46

THE GOSPEL OF JOHN 48

　Loving to the very end (John 13:1–38) 51

SAINT PAUL 53

　The power of the resurrection 53

　The death and resurrection of Jesus (Philippians 2:5–11) 55

　The new creation (Romans 5:12–21) 57

THE NEW TESTAMENT IN OUR CHRISTIAN LIVES 59

AN EXERCISE IN *LECTIO DIVINA* 61

GLOSSARY 64

FOREWORD

The pages that follow attempt to introduce a first-time reader, or a reader with only a passing acquaintance, to the two-thousand-year-old richness of the Church's New Testament. A better understanding can make us more familiar with the source and inspiration of what the Christian Churches do and teach.

In the first part of the book I outline some background to the New Testament, and then ask how this particular collection of books, known to us as the New Testament, came into existence. It is interesting to see how we finished up with just twenty-seven books, chosen from among dozens of others that were available and read in the early Church.

The second part of the book offers an introduction to the four Gospels, and to the person and teaching of Saint Paul. These are the texts more often used, and which are read to us within the Christian liturgies. It is best to focus our attention there, rather than saying something about the purpose and message of all twenty-seven books, some of which we seldom use or hear.

By way of conclusion, I ask about the use of the New Testament in the life and prayer of the Church. Finally, I offer an example of how a passage from the New Testament can be used in a form of prayer that has been alive in the Church for 1500 years, the practice of *Lectio Divina*: a meditative and prayerful reflection upon the Divine Word.

Francis J Moloney, SDB

Lynne Muir

INTRODUCTION

I spent several years teaching in the United States of America. One of the lasting impressions I have of the people I met there was their curiosity. Many times, while travelling or in other social settings, I was asked, 'What do you do for a living?' It was never enough to say I was a Catholic priest who taught in a university. That response only invited further curiosity, so I would have to admit that my life was dedicated to the study and teaching of the New Testament. 'You mean the Bible?' Yes, that was what I meant. It was a surprise to many that I could spend my life with only a part of the Bible, that part written in the Christian era.

I can understand that, as the Bible is so well known 'by name'. It is seen in bookshops, and found in hotel rooms all over the world. But how many are aware that it is a large collection of *different* books, starting with the book of Genesis and ending with the book of Revelation? Indeed, the Greek word *biblia*, from which we have our word 'Bible', means 'books'. The earlier and larger part of the Bible (the Old Testament, in the sense that it was written first and is thus 'older') was written across the millennium before Jesus came into the world (from about 1000 BC). The more recent section (the New Testament, written later and thus 'newer') was written in the decades following the life, death and resurrection of Jesus of Nazareth (from about AD 50–100).

A collection of different books written in different times, places and languages more than two thousand years ago takes some understanding. I have spent forty years of my life working at it, and I still have a lot to learn!

For some, the Gospels, the Letters of St Paul and the other

Susan Daily

documents in the New Testament are texts they have come to know through the practice of reading them with the family or in private. For those who go to a Christian Church regularly, they are familiar stories and exhortations that are read in Church. For many, however, they are documents written a long time ago that may be quaintly interesting, but have little or nothing to say to us or to the world we live in. Most people, we must admit, know nothing about them!

Yet wherever we go, we will find allusions to these texts. Many images that surround us come from the pages of the New Testament, especially the cross – ever popular in fashion items and as a body marking. Much of our classical, modern and contemporary art uses images that come from the New Testament, especially the image of mother and child, but also images of biblical episodes and the lives of the saints and martyrs. Some of our expressions, used without reflection, have their origins there. It was Pilate who first washed his hands of the innocent blood of Jesus (see Matt 27:24). Now we simply say, 'I wash my hands of that.'

These allusions, however, are found in mainstream culture and language because for almost 2000 years Christian traditions determined everyday life in much of the Western world and the new world of Africa and the Americas. What exactly is this book – or better, collection of smaller books – that we call the New Testament? Why has it been so influential for more than 2000 years? Does it still have anything to say to us? In this book I will do my best to unravel answers to these questions.

4

UNDERSTANDING BIBLE REFERENCES

The bible is referred to by naming the book, the chapter, and then the verse, in that order. For the books with shorter names, it is easy: e.g. Mark, John. The name of the book is generally provided in full. Longer names are abbreviated: e.g. Jeremiah becomes Jer and Matthew becomes Matt. The names and their abbreviations are provided at the beginning of your Bible. The Old Testament books are gathered together in the first part of the Bible and the New Testament in the second part of the Bible. They are also listed separately in the front of your Bible. Thus, Mark 8:22 means the Gospel of Mark, chapter 8, verse 22. It is found in the section of the Bible that contains the New Testament. The chapters and verses are clearly printed in the Bible. Similarly, Jer 40:12 means Jeremiah, chapter 40, verse 12. This passage will be found in the first part of your Bible, known to Christians as the Old Testament.

DID YOU KNOW

Many sayings in everyday use have their origins in the bible?
Here are a few:

Going the extra mile   Matthew 5:41
The salt of the earth   Matthew 5:13
Casting pearls before swine   Matthew 7:6
A wolf in sheep's clothing   Matthew 7:15
United we stand, divided we fall   Matthew 12:25
The blind leading the blind   Matthew 15:14
The eleventh hour   Matthew 20:6
Physician heal thyself   Luke 4:23
Eat drink and be merry   Luke 12:19
The prodigal returns   Luke 15:11-32
It is more blessed to give than to receive   Acts 20:35
The powers that be   Rom 13:1

The world of the New Testament

Judaism

No matter how much good will I might have, reading the New Testament is difficult. It is not like any other book, and it can be hard to understand. Indeed, there are places which appear impossible. This is the case because the books found in the New Testament were written 2000 years ago. They were written in a time, a place and a language that is foreign to us. We need to have some idea of the worlds that lie behind the writing of the books of the New Testament.

Jesus was a Jew, and so were his first disciples. The name Jesus Christ, so familiar to us as if it were his family name, really means that Jesus of Nazareth was the expected Messiah of Israel (see 2 Sam 7:12–15; Psalm 89:3–4). The Judaism of the first century was complex. It was the product of a long history that looked back to Abraham as the father of the nation, and Moses as the one who freed Israel from the slavery of Egypt and to whom God gave the law.

David was the remembered hero, and the Messiah would be from the house of David. But the royal line disappeared and the nation had suffered great

Susan Daily

losses and exile. The land was no longer theirs. Acts of heroism a few centuries before the Christian era led to the re-establishment of Israel, but it soon fell into division and faithlessness. In the time of Jesus and the early Church, there was no independent Israel. It was ruled by Rome through the agency of a puppet royalty, and was eventually destroyed in AD 70. Judaism has always been marked by people of great holiness and loyalty (prophets and kings). However, there were times when the God of Israel and his commandments were remembered only by a remnant.

In the time of Jesus and the earliest Christians there were many ways of being a Jew, just as today there are many ways in which people accept the Christian faith. In those days Sadducees, Pharisees, Zealots, Essenes and Christians, to mention just the best known groups, lived side by side and practised a common faith. Belief in the one true God and the observance of his commandments stood at the centre of this faith. But that observance was understood in different ways, often shaped by the history that gave birth to those various expressions of Judaism. Nevertheless, Judaism had its history, interpreted and told in what

> **JEWISH HOPE WAS BASED ON THE UNSHAKEABLE BELIEF THAT GOD WOULD INTERVENE.**

Lynne Muir

we know as the Old Testament; it had its law, its traditions and its land. Jesus lived and died at a time when these fundamentals of the Jewish way of life and hope were under threat.

There were different ways of understanding how God would resolve this threat and restore the land, how the law should be observed and how a community that lived by the law and its traditions should act. One way was known as 'messianism', that is, the hope for a Messiah. But not everyone expected a Messiah. The hopes of a saving figure that God would raise up from among the people fluctuated, depending upon the socio-political situation of Israel at any given time. At the time of Jesus there were hopes for a Messiah who might be a soldier Messiah of the line of David. But there were also hopes for a Messianic Priest. Some hoped for a combination of both.

Above all, Jewish hope was based on the unshakeable belief that God would intervene at the end of time, destroying all evil and restoring the original glory and beauty of his creation, lost because of human sin and evil. In the end, God will reign over all. We need to keep this in mind when we read, or hear the words 'the Kingdom of God'.

DID YOU KNOW

- △ the Sadducees and Pharisees lived Judaism differently?
- △ there was no such notion as a suffering and dying Messiah until Jesus began to speak in that way?
- △ both Jews and Christians believe that God made all things perfectly, and will restore perfection at the end of time?

The Greco-Roman world

The Jewish world described above did not exist in a vacuum. Israel existed as an independent nation for little more than two centuries. The nation was forever under siege, and conquered by the Assyrians and the Babylonians. The people were subjected to the Persians, and Israel was eventually swept into the Hellenistic Empire, which had its origins in Alexander the Great. Alexander was an incredible leader who lived from 356 till 323 BC. He conquered almost the whole of the known world before dying at just 33 years of age! He believed the Greek language and culture of his time (known as Hellenism) were so significant that they should be accepted and used by the whole world.

Well before the time of Jesus, Greek influence existed in Israel. Already some two centuries before Jesus Christ many Jews no longer understood enough Hebrew to read the sacred books and it was translated into Greek. The Greek Bible is called the Septuagint, based on a legend that it was translated simultaneously by seventy translators. The New Testament itself, most of which was written in the first century, is in Greek.

After Alexander, his generals fought over the Hellenistic Empire, and Israel passed from the Hellenistic rulers in Egypt (known as the Ptolemies) to the Hellenistic rulers in Syria (known as the Seleucids). Greek culture and the Greek language permeated Jewish life. It is most likely Jesus spoke Aramaic and some Greek.

After a brief period of independence, due to the victory of Israel over the Hellenistic empire of Syria in the Maccabean wars (early in the second century BC), the growth of the Roman Empire swallowed Israel. The birth and development of Christianity as a world religion owes much to the Roman Empire. Christianity came into existence during the high point of Roman rule, a period referred to as the Roman peace (the pax Romana). Peaceful conditions dominated the Roman system in so far as local administrations were allowed to continue as long as the Roman dominion was not threatened. This system accompanied the beginnings of a new world religion. The books of the New Testament reflect a believing community moving freely into the world beyond Judaism.

As the Hellenistic powers faded and the Roman Empire took over, new religions emerged. This was a time when the established religions were losing their attraction. The classical Greek religions were fading, helped by the fact that the Romans did not come with new religions

Lynne Muir

THE BIRTH AND DEVELOPMENT OF CHRISTIANITY AS A WORLD RELIGION OWES MUCH TO THE ROMAN EMPIRE.

Susan Daily

of their own. They tended to adapt the fading Greek religions and use them as they saw fit. Alexander the Great eventually declared himself to be a 'son of God', and subsequently the Roman Emperors had themselves proclaimed as 'gods' and demanded emperor worship.

The people hungered for a way to God, for salvation. They developed miracle stories and miraculous locations. Most important in this 'hunger for God' was the development of the mystery religions and Gnosticism. The New Testament was written in a world where these religions had captured the hearts and minds of many. They were religions into which specially privileged and enlightened people entered, assured of salvation through contact with, or knowledge of, the gods. Such religious thinking was foreign to Judaism, but very much a part of the world that saw the birth of Christianity and the writing of the New Testament.

DID YOU KNOW

△ although the Roman system of government was often harsh, the peace and order which ensued initially aided the spread of Christianity?

△ the Gnostics and those who entered the mystery religions sought an answer to the mystery of human longing?

How did the New Testament come into existence?

First things first

Have you ever noticed that we all have an interest in where people and things come from? When we meet people for the first time, we are interested in discovering the nation they are from, their city, their education, their parents and so on. The question about where the New Testament comes from is a good place for us to start. Let us trace where the twenty-seven 'books' that make up the New Testament came from.

The New Testament had its beginnings in the life and teaching of Jesus of Nazareth. He was a man like us, who lived across the first thirty years of the Christian era. It is not only Christians who tell us of Jesus' life and teaching. A number of non-Christians from the early centuries mention him in their writings. Some of these writings come from times very close to the time of Jesus and the earliest Church.

From the start, even before Jesus died, those who heard him remembered what he had said. His parables were especially memorable. They also remembered what he did, and recalled the incredible authority he had over sickness and evil. They remembered

Susan Daily

Jesus had told them that he was bringing in a new era, a time when God would reign in their hearts, minds and lives as their king. They remembered that in both his teaching and in his very personality, there were clear signs that the Kingdom of God was at hand. Not everyone believed in him. Indeed, the Romans and the Jews joined together to crucify him. Crucifixion was a Roman form of execution. But, the first Christians claimed he had been raised from the dead.

For decades, these 'memories' remained unwritten. The early Christians encouraged one another in difficulty; they gathered for prayer and remembered things that Jesus had said and done. But there was no need for any 'story' of Jesus. They knew it. They had either been with Jesus (a minority of people, the Twelve, and probably some other followers, including significant women, among them his mother), or had at least known him (the majority of people whose villages and homes he visited). One thing they all knew about was that he had been crucified!

The crucifixion of Jesus is an event reported in the writings of non-Christians. It was a regular Roman way of eliminating in an excruciatingly cruel way anyone who threatened their authority, or the very worst of criminals. Only about twenty years after the death of Jesus, St Paul described the difficulties of the early Christians. He was especially

> THE DEATH AND
> RESURRECTION
> OF JESUS
> MIGHT HAVE HAPPENED
> AT THE END
> OF JESUS' LIFE,
> BUT THEY WERE
> THE HEART
> OF THE EARLIEST
> CHRISTIAN MESSAGE.

Lynne Muir

concerned with his own task as someone who preached Jesus as the Christ. He writes to the Christians in Corinth: 'We preach a Christ crucified, a stumbling block to Jews and a folly to the Gentiles' (1 Cor 1:23).

No Jew could accept that the expected Christ could have been crucified, and Greeks would regard any such message as quite silly. Many who had originally followed Jesus would have decided that he could not be the Christ, but others remained firm in their faith. How did they overcome the scandal of the cross? This was the very first problem that the earliest Christians had to handle, but they did not have to do it on their own. They had experiences, and accepted a message that the cross was not the end of the story for Jesus. Jesus had always trusted in his Father, and his Father entered the story after the crucifixion by raising Jesus from the dead. Jesus had died on a Roman cross, but the cross was now empty. First things first: the experience of his death and the accepted message of his resurrection were at the heart of the earliest Christian message.

DID YOU KNOW

△ crucifixion was a Roman form of execution used to maintain social order?
△ Jesus' cruel death on a cross was the most difficult scandal the Christians had to face?
△ without Jesus' death and resurrection, Christianity is an empty religion?

Teaching before stories – Saint Paul

To the best of our knowledge, the first person to begin a tradition of writing about Jesus was Paul of Tarsus. He was also known as Saul, a well-trained and committed believing Jew to the extent that he collaborated in the persecution of the earliest Christians in Jerusalem and the surrounding regions. The Acts of the Apostles tell of a remarkable conversion experience he had while on a journey to Damascus. Paul himself does not mention the journey, but he regularly comes back to a transforming experience. He insists that he has been overcome and transformed by 'the power of the resurrection' (Phil 3:10).

Like any believing Jew, the idea that Jesus of Nazareth could have been the Christ would have been discounted by Saul of Tarsus. After all, he had been hung upon a tree, and this had already been described in the Old Testament as a curse (Deut 27:26; see Gal 3:13). The message was also abroad that Jesus had been raised from the dead. What these Christians were claiming for a man who had been crucified as a criminal was a stumbling block for any Jew. Saul wanted to ensure that such teaching would not take root and corrupt any of his fellow Jews.

Not everyone had been as well instructed as he had, and they might be tempted to believe that the scandal of the cross had been overcome by God by means of a resurrection. This had never been heard of, and he did not want anyone to be caught up in such fairy tales. A thousand years of Israelite religious history and his expert formation as a Pharisee were under threat with this new teaching. We can easily understand why Paul originally joined the opposition to this new-fangled religion based on a message that the man who had been crucified by the Romans had been raised, and was in some way 'alive' among those who believed in him and tried to follow his teaching. Paul's passion for the God of Israel could not tolerate this betrayal.

Something happened to Saul of Tarsus that transformed him into the greatest of the early Apostles; the first person to write about Jesus of Nazareth, and what it meant to believe in him and follow him. Paul did not have a 'conversion' as we understand that word. His passion for the God of Israel always drove him. He now found that God had made himself known in the crucified and risen Jesus of Nazareth. He never lost his love for his people and their God. He wonders why they cannot see that their God has been made known in and through Jesus Christ (see Romans 9–11).

Paul does not tell us 'the story' about the birth, life and teaching of Jesus. From the Letters of Paul, we know that 'when the time had fully come, God sent forth his Son, born of a woman, born under the law' (Gal 4:4). Paul is not interested

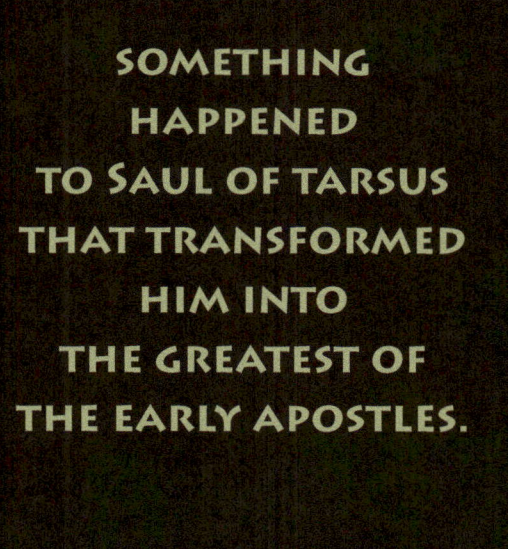

SOMETHING HAPPENED TO SAUL OF TARSUS THAT TRANSFORMED HIM INTO THE GREATEST OF THE EARLY APOSTLES.

Susan Daily

in the mother of Jesus. But he wants to insist that Jesus was fully human, born of a woman like all of us, and born under the Law of Moses. In Jewish thought and practice, 'Jewishness' is carried by one's mother. Paul insists, therefore, that Jesus was born of a Jewish mother. But this person, who was born into the world like all of us and shared our humanity with us, was also God's Son.

In writing to the Corinthians, Paul reminds them that they must not be selfish and interested in their own lives while neglecting those less blessed. He reminds them of something he had heard and had passed on to them. The night before Jesus died he celebrated a meal with his disciples that transformed Jewish Passover practices. Jesus told his disciples that he was giving his body and his blood to form a new covenant. They were to give their own bodies and shed their own blood in memory of him. Every time they were to do this, they would be proclaiming Jesus until such time as he came back again (see 1 Cor 11:17-34).

Finally, Paul dwells throughout his letters on the obedience of Jesus, supremely manifested in Jesus' death, and God's response, manifested in Jesus' resurrection. But Paul tells of those events in another passage in 1 Corinthians where he reminds his readers of another story that he had heard and then passed on to them. Jesus had been crucified and buried, yet raised from the dead and seen by a number of witnesses, even by Paul (see 1 Cor 15:1-8). Jesus crucified and Jesus risen – this is the message that lies at the heart of Paul's teaching.

DID YOU KNOW

△ Paul would have always regarded himself as a Jew?
△ Paul's belief in the God of Israel never weakened?
△ Jesus' death and resurrection shows the 'power' of God's love?

The stories – the Gospels

For the first Christians, the memory of Jesus' life, teaching, death and resurrection was still powerfully alive. Paul did not tell it, but with the passing of time and the gradual spread of the Christian communities beyond the Judaism of Palestine into the larger Greco-Roman world, a question began to emerge: 'Who was this man, Jesus of Nazareth, whom you Christians regard as the Christ, the Son of God?'

The best way to answer that question, some believed, was to tell his story. As Christians gathered for the celebration of a special meal, they told the story of what Jesus had said and done 'on the night before he died'. Jesus, crucified and risen, continued to be with his followers, as they 'remembered' him in a way that made him present. The 'story' of Jesus' celebration of a meal, the beginning of the Eucharistic meals that are still the central celebration of the Christian community, is told (Mark 14:22–26; Matt 26:26–29; Luke 22:15–20; 1 Cor 11:25–26), or alluded to (Mark 6:31–44; 8:1–10; Matt 14:13–21; 15:32–39; Luke 9:10–17; John 6:51–58; 13:1–38) in many parts of the New Testament.

Another 'story' that was told from the very beginnings of Christianity was the story of Jesus' passion, death and resurrection. The fact that Jesus was crucified as a criminal was a challenge to all who followed him as the Christ and the Son of God. The narratives of Jesus' final night with his disciples, his prayer in Gethsemane, his arrest, his trial before Jewish and

Susan Daily

Roman authorities, his crucifixion and death, the discovery of an empty tomb three days after the crucifixion, and a number of encounters between the disciples and the risen Jesus are very old. All the Gospels tell this particular 'story' in the same sequence. This does not happen anywhere else in the Gospels. The passion and resurrection stories never change because they were told this way from the beginning. The early Christians boldly told the story over and over again, explaining what each event and each moment meant for Jesus, and for them.

Of course, many other stories are found in the Gospels. We cannot be sure whether there were some narratives about the life of Jesus available in written form before the Gospel of Mark appeared in about AD 70. There were many 'stories' of Jesus' alive in the early Christian communities. The parables must have rung in the ears, minds and hearts of the original listeners, and they would have been told over and over again as the generations passed. But there was no single 'story of Jesus' told from beginning to end, existing in written form.

Very few people could read or write. What we call 'oral tradition', the passing on of stories from the life and teaching of Jesus would have been a major part of the sharing of faith among those first believers. They would have encouraged one another in times of difficulty, instructed their children, spoken about Jesus to their friends and told stories to those whom they wanted to draw into their community of faith. Eventually, a large number of so-called 'gospels' came to be written for use in the communities. Those few who could read and write provided a story of Jesus to be read by very

> As Christians gathered for the celebration of a special meal, they told the story of what Jesus had said and done ' on the night before he died'. Jesus, crucified and risen, continued to be with his followers, as they 'remembered' him in a way that made him present.
>
> Susan Daily

few, but listened to by the vast majority.

To this day we have many 'gospels' that are not found in the New Testament. You may have heard of some of them: the Gospel of Phillip, the Gospel of Judas and the Gospel of Mary. By the middle of the second century, four of the many 'gospels' were accepted, continuing the practice of telling stories about the great figures of the past that forms a major part of the Old Testament. They were read in the Church as part of the Christian Scriptures. The four Gospels are the Gospel of Mark (written about AD 70), Matthew (written about AD 85), Luke (written about AD 85) and John (written about AD 100).

DID YOU KNOW

△ we all have stories that are never written, but are alive among our families and friends?

△ a Gospel is a story of the life, teaching, death and resurrection of Jesus?

△ the word 'Gospel' comes from old English and means 'good news'?

△ each of the Gospels tells the story of Jesus in a slightly different way?

Pauline writings in the New Testament

We regularly hear the name 'Paul' associated with 2 Thessalonians, Colossians, Ephesians, Titus, 1 Timothy, 2 Timothy and even the Letter to the Hebrews. This is understandable, as the authors of these documents, with the exception of Hebrews, claim that they were written by Paul. On the basis of that claim, they are proclaimed in the liturgical life of the Christian Churches as letters of Paul. But there are good reasons for suspecting that Paul was not the author of all these letters.

1 and 2 Thessalonians

Both 1 and 2 Thessalonians deal with the problem of the end of the world and the attitude believers must have as they wait for that time to come. But there are some strange differences. 2 Thessalonians 2:1–12 claims that there are some who believe the day of the Lord has already come, and the author responds to this by a description of that time. We do not find this anywhere else in Paul. The author seems to go out of his way to insist that he is 'Paul'. He says it twice and insists on his authority (1:1; 2:1; 3:14–15, 17), unlike his other letters. It seems that he protests too much and this arouses suspicion. It is possible, but not likely, that 2 Thessalonians was written very shortly after 1 Thessalonians to the same people in the same situation of anxiety about the final coming of the Lord. It is better explained as a later 'imitation' of the authentically 'Pauline' 1 Thessalonians, but addressing a different situation.

Scholars use the expression 'Pauline writings' to mean those letters found in the New Testament that were either written by Paul or have been attributed to Paul, and 'Pauline tradition' to refer to that theological tradition, with its central focus on the death and resurrection of Jesus that has its origins in the teaching of Paul.

Colossians and Ephesians

Colossians develops a rich theology of creation, and God's saving presence in Jesus Christ, the high point and perfection of all creation. The inspiring theology of salvation and creation arises from the problems the author is addressing. It is most evident in Colossians 2:8–23. The author opposes a 'philosophy of empty deceit', the result of 'human tradition' and the 'elemental spirits of the universe' (v 8). The author seems to be dealing with a false way of understanding the world that puts Christ in a position lower than some system of elemental spirits. This cannot be accepted, as only Christ is the universal and cosmic redeemer. The Greco-Roman world provides the setting and background for such teaching.

What must be recognised, of course, is that this understanding of Jesus Christ does not change from Paul's fundamental point of view. It is being transported into a later time and place. Similarly, although the situation has changed, the author continues the Pauline tradition that no human system can bring about the salvation of humankind. In this letter, the author can point to the uselessness of Jewish ceremonial law, taboos and calendar observances (see 2:16–18, 20–22). Only one thing matters: 'holding fast to the Head, from whom the whole body, nourished and knit together through its joints and ligaments, grows with a growth that is from God.' The importance of oneness in Christ is found throughout the Pauline letters, but Paul never quite says it like this.

Ephesians also seems to reflect a time later than Paul. The anguish that Paul reveals in his concern over the final salvation of the Jews in Romans 9–11 has disappeared. The author develops a magnificent theology of the unity of the Church. The hostility between Jew and Greek ends because of Jesus' death. It is not as if this subject is non-Pauline. Indeed, it is a clear continuation of Paul's understanding of Jesus' death (see Rom 15:5–6). However, he has never before approached this subject in this way.

Both Colossians and Ephesians begin to show a concern for the right order of the Christian household (see Col 3:18–4:1; Eph 5:21–6:9). Paul's never-failing insistence on love (see especially 1 Cor 13) is behind these more practical recommendations. But as with other issues faced in these two beautiful letters, Paul does not deal with the question of love as it is dealt with in later letters.

THE GIFT OF LOVE

If I speak in the tongues of mortals and of angels, but do not have love, I am a noisy gong or a clanging cymbal. And if I have prophetic powers, and understand all mysteries and all knowledge, and if I have all faith, so as to remove mountains, but do not have love, I am nothing. If I give away all my possessions, and if I hand over my body so that I may boast, but do not have love, I gain nothing.

Love is patient; love is kind; love is not envious or boastful or arrogant or rude. It does not insist on its own way; it is not irritable or resentful; it does not rejoice in wrongdoing, but rejoices in the truth. It bears all things, believes all things, hopes all things, endures all things.

Love never ends. But as for prophecies, they will come to an end; as for tongues, they will cease; as for knowledge, it will come to an end. For we know only in part, and we prophesy only in part; but when the complete comes, the partial will come to an end. When I was a child, I spoke like a child, I thought like a child, I reasoned like a child; when I became an adult, I put an end to childish ways. For now we see in a mirror, dimly, but then we will see face to face. Now I know only in part; then I will know fully, even as I have been fully known. And now faith, hope, and love abide, these three; and the greatest of these is love.

1 Cor 13

Lynne Muir

DID YOU KNOW

△ it was customary in antiquity to claim a famous person as being the author of a book, even if that person was dead?

△ claiming authorship by a famous person was done out of love and loyalty to that person and his or her message?

The Pastoral Epistles

The letters to Titus and 1 and 2 Timothy also claim to come from Paul. They are written at a time when the Churches addressed by these documents are well established communities, beginning to feel the strain which always emerges as a developing group must cope with its human frailty. How leaders are to behave; how elders, widows and slaves are to be treated; and how to distinguish between heresy and right teaching are important issues that did not overly bother Paul during his career.

These documents, generally well described as the 'Pastoral Epistles', probably date from the end of the first century or early in the second century. Paul had been dead for some forty years, but his message still had to be passed on to a new and different generation of Christians.

There are issues and arguments in the documents that do not appear to be authentically Pauline. The argument, the style and even the choice of words in these letters are not found in the seven epistles that are universally regarded as written by Paul. Secondly, in antiquity it was quite common to use the name of a significant figure from the past as the author of a document, especially when that figure remained the inspiration for the actual author. These letters, which look back to Paul for their authority, are an example of a widespread practice in antiquity known as 'pseudonymity'. We must be careful not to apply our twenty-first century criteria to judge this widely used practice because 2 Thessalonians, Colossians, Ephesians, Titus and 1 and 2 Timothy all continue the

Lynne Muir

Pauline tradition and are the inspired Word of God.

Whoever the authors were, they made the Pauline understanding of God, Christ, the Christian and the community of the Christian Church their own. They do not betray Paul; they have taken Paul's message to heart. They apply it to later times and later situations. Tensions within different groups in the community were felt; problems concerning correct or false interpretation and teaching of what God had done in Jesus and how they were to live as a consequence of that were emerging. Christian communities were facing strange but sometimes fascinating religious teaching and practices coming from the Greco-Roman world.

Paul's authentic letters

Paul's authentic letters were written to specific groups in the earliest Church (remember Paul had been martyred by the mid-sixties). He did not have to face the internal and external problems that Christians faced later in the first century. The letters Paul certainly wrote are 1 Thessalonians (written from Corinth about AD 50), Galatians, 1 Corinthians, 2 Corinthians, Philemon, Philippians (all written during a long stay in Ephesus from AD 54–57) and Romans (written from Corinth in AD 58). Inspired by that heritage, the later letters claim the authority of Paul by their steady reference to him as the 'author'. He is their author in so far as he is their 'author-ity'.

> PAUL HAD BEEN DEAD SOME FORTY YEARS, BUT HIS MESSAGE STILL HAD TO BE PASSED ON TO A NEW AND DIFFERENT GENERATION OF CHRISTIANS.

Susan Daily

Letter to the Hebrews

The Letter to the Hebrews does not claim to be Pauline, but it is often associated with Paul. Indeed, this document is more a theological tract or a sermon than a letter. In an elegant and subtle fashion, it argues that all God's former institutions and means of communication with humankind have been perfected in Jesus Christ. The new covenant was foreshadowed in the Law of Moses and came to reality only in the person and work of Jesus. Hebrews has a unique literary form. It is a superb sample of Greek writing and was certainly not from the pen of Paul. It was probably written in the last decade of the first century.

DID YOU KNOW

△ not all the letters which claim to be written by Paul were actually written by him, some were written by people who loved and admired him?

△ authors who wrote letters under the name of Paul wanted Paul's message to live on in a newer generation?

The remaining New Testament documents

The Catholic Epistles

The documents in the New Testament known as 1 and 2 Peter; 1, 2 and 3 John; the Epistle of James and the Epistle of Jude have been described from the earliest times as 'The Catholic Epistles'. The Greek word 'catholic' means 'general', and it was applied to these letters during the discussions of which books written over the first decades of the Christian Church should be included among the Christian Scriptures. Several factors contributed to the linking of these seven epistles and their being called 'the Catholic Epistles'. They were identified by the name of the author (Peter, John, James and Jude). All other epistles in the Christian Scriptures (the letters of Paul and the Letter to the Hebrews) are known by their audience. They are also the only documents in the Christian Scriptures not attributed to Paul which have something approximating letter-form.

There are seven Catholic Epistles, just as there are twice seven (fourteen) letters accepted by tradition as Pauline (including Hebrews). Within Revelation there are seven 'letters to the Churches' (Rev 2:1–3:22). The regular appearance of 'seven' associated with letters in early Christianity may be one of the reasons why such very brief documents as 2 and 3 John and Jude have been included, and have maintained their place within the Christian

Susan Daily

Canon. The number 'seven', which is significant in many cultures, has its own biblical background (see, for example, Gen 2:1–3; 4:24; 41:2–36; Deut 7:1; Judges 16:14; Ruth 4:15; Josh 6:1–21). It has the meaning of totality, fullness and completeness. There was a sense in the second and third centuries, when the problem of which books were 'in' and which were 'out' (see next section), that this final 'seven' completed the collection.

Some very early writers had already called 1 John a 'Catholic Epistle', indicating that the letter was not directed to any particular Church. This use of the expression to describe 1 John was a way of characterising the wide focus of the letter's address, especially when compared to the very specific focus of 2 and 3 John. It is clear that 2 and 3 John were directed to a specific Church (2 John 1: 'the elect lady'; 3 John 1: 'Gaius'), but their close association with 1 John also links them with the idea of being 'catholic', that is, for everyone. 1 Peter addresses 'the exiles of the Dispersion in Pontus, Galatia, Cappadocia, Asia, and Bithynia' (1 Peter 1:1), and that all-embracing description can be regarded as 'catholic'. The recipients of James are not identified, and Jude and 2 Peter are addressed to all Christians. The original meaning of 'catholic' can be justifiably applied to them. These letters, especially the Letter of James and 1 Peter, contain teaching that is both moving and fundamental to Christian life and practice.

Revelation

The final book in our New Testament is widely known as 'the Apocalypse', but is sometimes also called 'Revelation'. In fact, both names mean the same thing: 'apocalypse' is a Greek word for 'revelation'. Most readers would regard this book as the most obscure text in the New Testament. The reasons for its obscurity must be understood. A lack of understanding of what the author of Revelation, known as 'John', was trying to say, and the 'literary form' he used to convey his message, has led to many wild uses of the sometimes fantastic images in the book. It is used by fanatics who read into it all sorts of prophecies about the future of the world, and it is read by some fundamentalist sectarians who apply certain images to organisations they despise (for example, the whore of Babylon in Revelation 17 is identified as the Catholic Church). The use of numbers are similarly abused (for example, the number 666 in Revelation 13:18, representing the Antichrist, has been variously applied to a medieval Pope, Adolf Hitler and Ronald Reagan).

Revelation has many fellow travellers, written about the same time. It belongs to a literary genre called 'apocalyptic'. Apocalyptic books were especially common within Judaism over those times when the nation and its religious practice were under threat. When the forces that opposed them were humanly so overpowering, the authors of apocalyptic literature turned to God. It may appear that there is no human hope, but the action of God will bring an end to this corrupt and violent enemy, and restore the fortunes of God's people. However, if God is the chief agent in the 'narrative', then the story must be full of symbols and puzzling encounters between heaven and earth. One cannot speak of the action of God as one speaks of the actions of human beings. This is the case with Revelation. Looking at extermination at the hands of the Roman persecutors, John the elder inspires hope and faithfulness in God. The wonders contain a powerful message of the victory of the lamb who was slain. Unless Revelation is read in this way, it is inevitably 'mis-read'.

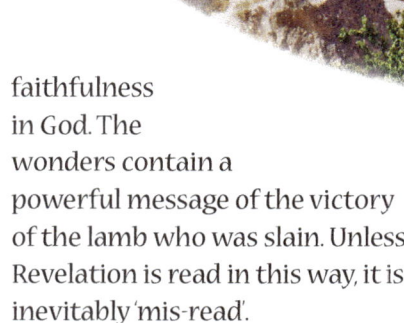

Lynne Muir

DID YOU KNOW

△ the word 'catholic' means 'everyone' and not a Church?
△ Christians used the word 'catholic' long before it was used to mean the Catholic Church?

THE NEW TESTAMENT EMERGES

Already at the end of the second century, a document written in Rome in wretched Latin (probably a translation from Greek), indicates that there was a 'collection' of Christian documents that formed a Christian Bible, like the Jewish Bible. This document, called 'the Muratorian Fragment' lists the four Gospels, Acts, and the Pauline letters. However, Hebrews, 1 and 2 Peter, 3 John and James are absent. A 'New Testament' had begun to take shape. But it contained other early Christian documents that eventually did not 'make it' into the collection. A process of 'collecting' was no doubt under way, but what was 'in' or 'out' was far from certain.

A Greek Father of the Church, Origen (ca 185 – ca 254), and the Church's earliest 'historian', Eusebius (260 – ca 340), had devised a three-fold classification of Christian books. Some were regarded as 'certainly canonical', others 'still debated' and a third group was to be 'rejected'. For Origen, whose authority was very great, 1 Peter and 1 John already belonged to the 'certain', but 2 Peter, 2 and 3 John, James and Jude were still 'debated'. However, none of them were 'rejected'. For Origen there was still a deal of uncertainty. He had great respect for some documents that did not eventually become part of the New Testament, for example, the Epistle of Barnabas and the Didache.

The collection of books was called a 'canon'. This expression originally meant some kind of 'measuring rod' and then a 'rule' you could live by. Eventually it led to the acceptance of the idea of a collection of accepted books. The expression is not limited to its use as 'the Christian Canon', or 'the Jewish Canon,' in reference to the books of the Bible. It is also used, for example, to speak of the 'canon' of what should be regarded as classical English Literature. But it had its origin as the description of

Date	Event	Book
4 BC—AD 30	Life of Jesus	
	Ministry	
	Death	
	Resurrection	
	Birth of the Early Church	
AD 31	Conversion of Saul	
AD 31—64	Paul's Journeys and Ministry	
AD 51		1 Thessalonians
AD 53—54		1 Corinthians
AD 55		II Corinthians
AD 56		Philippians
AD 56		Galatians
AD 56—57		Romans
AD 56—57		Philemon
AD 64—68	Peter and Paul martyred	
AD 65—70		Gospel of Mark
AD 65—70		Colossians
AD 70	Destruction of Jerusalem	
AD 70—80		II Thessalonians
AD 70—80		Ephesians
AD 80—90		Gospel of Luke
AD 80—90		Acts of the Apostles
AD 85—90		Gospel of Matthew
AD 90—100		Gospel of John
AD 90—125		I Timothy
AD 90—125		II Timothy
AD 90—125		Titus

books that eventually made it into the Bible.

The canon was clearly hardening into a definite list in the fourth century. There is still fluidity, however, as one can see from the great written manuscripts that began to appear at this time. Two of the most complete and highly regarded ancient collections of the books of the New Testament (known as Sinaiticus and Alexandrinus) still contain some texts that were eventually excluded. The principles that led the Church to accept some Christian books into its 'Bible' and exclude others are hard to determine. Obviously, any document that claimed to go back to the Apostles was given great authority. Another practice that would have thrown certain documents into relief was their use in the liturgies of the Christian communities. They would have come to be known and loved. However, the most likely criterion that led to certain books being always present to the communities was that they were relevant! Some books seemed to speak to the human and spiritual needs of the believers. They emerged from a large sea of narratives, exhortations and letters as the ones that meant most to the people. I like to think of the books that we now have in our New Testament as hard diamonds that emerged from the morass (some of it sludge) of other early Christian documents.

We often hear (for example, in Dan Brown's *Da Vinci Code*) that Constantine and the authority of the Church imposed the books of the New Testament on the people. This is simply wrong. The people eventually determined which story of Jesus they wanted to hear, and which exhortations and teachings made sense of their lives of faith. The faithful told the Church what they wanted, and by the end of the fourth century, the New Testament was well on the way. The first clear statement on the books of the New Testament, as we have it today, is found in the writings of Saint Athanasius, a great figure from the Eastern Church. In his thirty-ninth Easter letter of 367, preserved for us almost completely in Greek, Syriac, and Coptic, which indicates how important Athanasius' words were, Athanasius named the twenty-seven books of our present New Testament as the only canonical books. The debate continued for a little longer in the West, but in 405 Pope Innocent I (Bishop of Rome from 401–417), in response to a question from the bishops in Gaul (today's France), repeated the list of Athanasius.

The Pope would have been influenced by two great Latin Fathers of the Church, Saint Jerome (331–420) and Saint Augustine (345–430) who had already accepted the New Testament of Athanasius.

The process sketched above is pastorally important. The contents of the New Testament did not emerge from decisions made by an Emperor or a Pope. Nor was anything said in the early Councils of the Church, however much they were familiar with the Gospels and the Letters of Paul. The early Councils used these documents often, and as ultimate authority to determine answers to difficult questions about God, Jesus Christ and Christian life.

Lynne Muir

Susan Daily

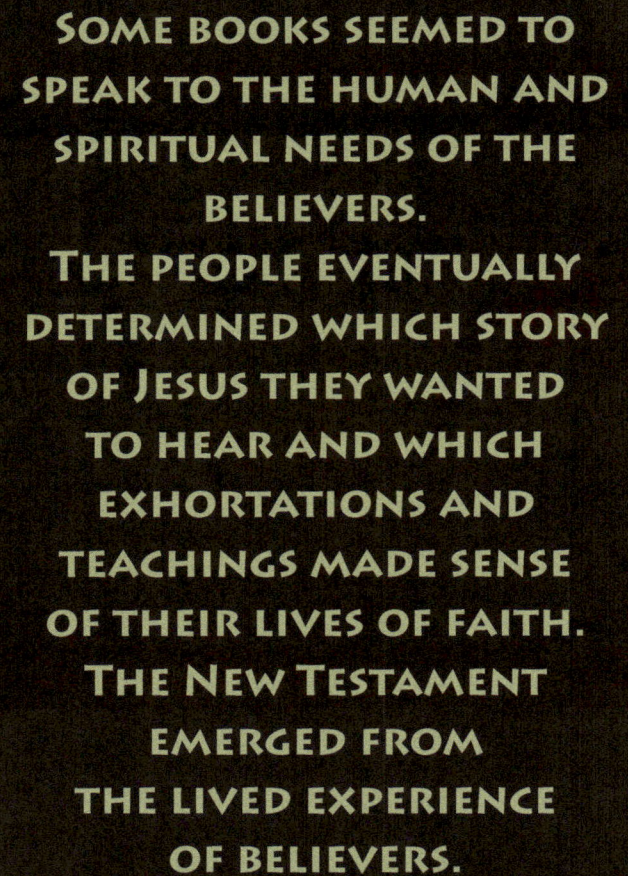

> Some books seemed to speak to the human and spiritual needs of the believers. The people eventually determined which story of Jesus they wanted to hear and which exhortations and teachings made sense of their lives of faith. The New Testament emerged from the lived experience of believers.

The New Testament emerged from the lived experience of the believers and was eventually articulated by their shepherds in response to their needs. This, after all, was the concern of the Letter of Athanasius in 367 and Innocent I's response to the Gallic bishops in 405. It often comes as a surprise to know that it was not until the Council of Florence, as the Churches of East and West debated their divisions and their union, that Athanasius' list was formally defined by the Roman Church as the Canon of the New Testament (1442). This decision was then ratified at the Council of Trent (8 April 1546), in the context of the same question raised by the Fathers of the Reformation: which books belong to the Bible? There is still a 'Catholic' and a 'Protestant' Bible as the Protestant tradition accepted into the Old Testament only texts that were available in Hebrew, while the Catholic tradition accepted several books that existed in the pre-Christian Greek Septuagint. The 27 documents listed by Athanasius in 367 as 'in' are accepted by Catholics and Protestants. The others, no matter how impressive they might appear, are 'out'.

DID YOU KNOW

- △ the books of the New Testament were the favourite books of the faithful people?
- △ the Protestant and Catholic Bibles are slightly different?

Jesus of Nazareth — A Biography

It probably comes as a surprise to hear that we do not have a life of Jesus as we would understand the 'life of' anyone. Each of the four Gospels tells its story of Jesus differently. They were not written to be read as a modern 'life of Jesus'. It might also be a surprise to know that the man we know as 'Jesus Christ' was never known by that name during his life. He was known as 'Jesus of Nazareth' (see especially Matt 2:23). He was probably also known as 'Jesus son of Joseph' (see John 1:45). These were names given to a person seen to be special, but only human, by all who knew him. The best we can do is trace the elements of his life by looking across the Gospels to find the outline of his story.

Jesus' story would look something like this. After his young life in Nazareth, about which we know little or nothing, he appeared on the scene at about 30 years of age. The infancy stories of Matthew 1–2 and Luke 1–2 deserve special attention and we will consider them on their own. Initially he was most likely a follower of John the Baptist, who may also have been related to him, as we hear in the Gospel of Luke (Luke 1:36). On some occasions John the Baptist speaks of Jesus as one who 'comes after him', probably indicating that he was his follower (see Mark 1:7; Matt 3:11; John 1:27). However, as the Baptist disappeared off the scene, arrested and eventually slain by Herod, Jesus began his own ministry, probably in Galilee (see John 3:22–24; Mark 12:14–15; Matt 4:12–17; Luke 4:14–15).

Jesus was a wandering preacher who brought much hope and love into a society that was oppressed by the presence of the Romans and exploited by the wealthy. As he began to preach about the coming of the reigning presence of God into the hearts and lives of all men and women, he quickly gathered many who followed him and placed their

Susan Daily

hopes in him. He was certainly seen as a prophet like the great prophets of Israel (see Mark 8:28; Matt 16:14; Luke 9:19; John 4:19, 44). He chose twelve disciples to journey with him (see Mark 3:13–14; Matt 10:2–4; Luke 6:12–13; John 6:70). There was probably also a larger group of friends who followed him, including women (see Luke 8:1–3), and many people in the villages and even the towns who looked to him with hope. Indeed, he became so popular that the Romans and even some Jewish authorities became concerned that he might cause trouble – arousing the people to rebellion (see John 11:47–48). They thought he might even be seen as the much-expected Messiah of Israel (see Mark 8:33; Matt 16:16; Luke 9:20; John 1:41).

Jesus was unhappy with any popular acclaim that he might be the expected Messiah. Throughout the Gospels he is cautious about any such acclamation. This was especially clear as he did not ride into Jerusalem on a war-horse with a sword in his hand to drive out the enemies of the true Israel (see Mark 11:1–10; Matt 21:1–9; Luke 19:28–38; John 12:12–19). Indeed, he began to speak of openness to God, to the need for unconditional love and obedience, even unto death (see Mark 8:34–9:1; Matt 16:24–28; Luke 9:13–27; John 13:1–21).

Jesus made it clear to his followers that he did not see death as the end of his story. He showed trust and confidence in God, whom he dared to call 'father' (see Mark 14:36). God would win through Jesus' death, and vindicate his suffering (Mark 8:31; 9:31; 10:32–34). Many of the disciples, and even the Twelve, found this difficult to accept, and the Gospels tell us, in their various ways, that one of them betrayed him, another denied him, and everyone else ran away. Jesus was crucified alone, the worst death the Romans

> **JESUS MADE IT CLEAR TO HIS FOLLOWERS THAT HE DID NOT SEE DEATH AS THE END OF HIS STORY.**

Susan Daily

could inflict upon anyone.

After three days women (maybe only one, Mary Magdalene [John 20:1-10]) found an empty tomb, and more and more people had an experience of the risen Jesus (1 Cor 15:3-8). He was alive! Now they began to understand that Jesus was the Messiah, but the Messiah that God wanted, not the one expected by popular culture. Now he could be called Jesus Christ. Many of the disciples gathered, their weakness was forgiven, they were promised they would continue his presence in the world in their meals, their prayers, their love, their hope and in their imitation of Jesus – prepared to be obedient to God unto death, confident that God would have the last word.

That is how 'the Church' began. It was not known by that name till much later. The death and resurrection of Jesus created a small community of fragile believers. They began to tell stories about his time among them, to celebrate the meal 'in memory of him', and they tried to live as he had taught them. Now deeper questions began to emerge. In the light of his death and resurrection, what was Jesus' relationship to the God of Israel whom he called 'father'? What was the gift of the Spirit he had promised would be with them? How had his death and resurrection offered a new life to humankind? It was out of all these thoughts, discussions, prayers, exhortations and stories that the New Testament was born.

DID YOU KNOW

△ Jesus only came to be known as 'Jesus Christ' after his death and resurrection?

△ the Gospels were never written as history books?

△ the authors wanted to tell what God did for us in and through Jesus Christ?

The Gospels

Matthew

Mark

Luke

John

When I was in primary school we were taught the names of the Gospels by learning to say together: 'Matthew, Mark, Luke and John, hold the horse while I get on.' Most people are aware that there are four Gospels, given the names of possible authors (Matthew, Mark, Luke and John) late in the second century. Those names were not attached to the original writing of the Gospels. We cannot be sure of the authors, but let's keep those names. They have served well for almost 2000 years, so we can stick with them, no matter who originally wrote each Gospel.

The synoptic Gospels

The Gospels are divided into two groups. Matthew, Mark and Luke are called 'synoptic Gospels'. This expression comes from the fact that by putting the three Gospels side by side, we can see that they closely compare with one another. They can be seen with one look of the eye. This is what is meant by the Greek word behind 'synoptic' (sun-opsis): 'with the eye'. This is not the case for the Gospel of John. The synoptic Gospels all begin Jesus' ministry in Galilee and have him eventually journey to Jerusalem. After a brief but intense ministry in Jerusalem he is eventually arrested, tried and killed. It is in Jerusalem that he dies and is raised. There are many places where Matthew, Mark and Luke tell the same story, in the same order as one another, and almost with the same words. Beware! This is not always the case, as we shall see. Matthew must be read as Matthew wanted his story to be read, and the same must be said for Mark and Luke.

Most likely, Mark's Gospel was written first (about AD 70). Matthew and Luke followed some

Susan Daily

time in the 80s; they probably had Mark in front of them, as they depend upon his order and often on his words, but there are places where they differ. Matthew and Luke did not follow Mark slavishly. Indeed, there are many places where Matthew and Luke have material from Jesus (especially his teaching) that is not found in Mark or John. They appear to have had another 'source', independent of Mark. This material has come to be known as 'Q', the first letter of the German word for 'source' (*Quelle*). As well as this special material from a common source, both Matthew and Luke had their own memories of Jesus, their own stories of Jesus told in their communities. Thus, there are stories and teachings of Jesus found only in Matthew and Luke, and there are stories and teachings of Jesus found only in Matthew and only in Luke.

What must never be forgotten, of course, is that for all the material that finished up in the written books, the communities and the authors looked back to their memories of Jesus of Nazareth. Now they understood more. In the light of the resurrection and in the life of the Spirit they were able to confidently claim that he was the Christ and the Son of God (see, for example, Mark 1:1; Matt 16:13–16; Luke 1:26–38; John 20:30–31). Jesus never used these terms to speak of himself. But now they were beginning to understand the full significance of what God did for humankind in and through Jesus.

Jesus as the pre-existent Logos

The Gospel of John is very different. Jesus is regularly in Jerusalem, especially for the celebrations of the great feasts (Pentecost [John 2], Sabbath [chapter 5], Passover [chapter 6],

BLESSED ARE THOSE WHO HAVE NOT SEEN YET BELIEVE.

JN 20:29

Susan Daily

Tabernacles [7:1–10:21] and Dedication [10:22–42]). Written at the end of the first Christian century (about AD 100), after more reflection, life in the Spirit and prayer, the understanding of Jesus as the Christ and the Son of God had developed even further. Though some of the stories from the synoptic Gospels reappear (for example, the multiplication of the loaves and fishes, the confession of Peter, and the passion story), the Jesus of the Gospel of John is different. He is presented as the pre-existent Logos (John 1:1–18). He knows all things and leads the believer – both the disciples in the story and the readers of the story – into an ever greater commitment of faith, so that everyone might believe more deeply that Jesus is the Christ, the Son of God, and have life because of this belief (see 20:30–31). 'Blessed are those who have not seen, yet believe' (20:29).

DID YOU KNOW

- △ the details of the life of Jesus in Matthew, Mark and Luke are sometimes different?
- △ Jesus' life in the Gospel of John is very different again?
- △ the main concern of the Gospel writers was to teach faith in God and Jesus Christ through their stories?

The Gospel of Mark

Let us start our reflection on the Gospels with the first to be written: the Gospel of Mark, written about AD 70. A careful reading of this Gospel, even for the beginner, reveals that Mark has designed his storytelling in two halves: Mark 1:1–8:30 and 8:31–16:8. As we read slowly and carefully through the various episodes in the first half of the Gospel a single question emerges: 'Who is Jesus?' It is asked by different people throughout (see 1:27, 37; 2:7, 16, 18; 3:6, 11–12, 20–22; 4:41; 5:16–17). The questioning comes to an end as Jesus finally asks his disciples at Caesarea Philippi, 'Who do people say that I am?' (8:27). Peter's answer to that question is, 'You are the Messiah' (8.29). This sounds fine to us – but not to Jesus. The section ends with Jesus warning his disciples severely not to talk about him in this way (8:30).

The second half of the Gospel opens with an immediate explanation of who Jesus is: the Son of Man who must go up to Jerusalem to suffer and to die, and to be raised on the third day (8:31). Jesus is the Messiah, but he will be a suffering, Son of Man, Messiah. The second half of the Gospel explains this further. On three occasions he is presented to his disciples as the suffering and raised Son of Man (8:31; 9:31; 10:32–34). As a result of his suffering he will take his place at the right hand of God and come at the end of time as the universal judge (8:38; 13:24–27; 14:61–62). During his passion, as they mock him, his opponents ask that he come down from his cross so that

Susan Daily

they might believe (15:29–32). They have not understood the nature of Jesus' messiahship. It is as the crucified and risen Son of Man that he is both Messiah and Son of God (see 1:1). To come down from the cross would be a denial of Jesus as Son of God and Messiah. It is the saving effect of God's action in Jesus' suffering, death and resurrection that makes sense of his story.

For this reason, as Jesus dies his agonising death on the cross, a Gentile, the Roman centurion, confesses: 'Truly, this man was the Son of God' (15:39). Three times across the Gospel, almost acting as 'sign posts' in the story, Jesus has been proclaimed 'Son of God': at the beginning by the voice from heaven (1:11), in the middle, again by a voice from heaven (9:7), and finally on the cross in his moment of death (15:39).

This way of obedience unto death so that God might enter his story and raise him from death (see 16:6) must be the measure of the life of all who claim to be Jesus' followers. In the Gospel of Mark there are two main characters: Jesus (of course) and the disciples. Each of his predictions in the second half of the Gospel (8:31, 9:31; 10:32–34) is directed to his disciples, to instruct them in what they must do if they are to 'follow' him (see 1:16–20). But they are never able to accept this challenge. They succeed reasonably well in the first half of the Gospel (see 6:6b–13), but in the second half their obtuseness becomes clear. They will not, or cannot, understand what it means to follow the crucified Messiah and Son of God.

The presentation of Jesus in the Gospel of Mark is strongly focused upon a suffering Jesus,

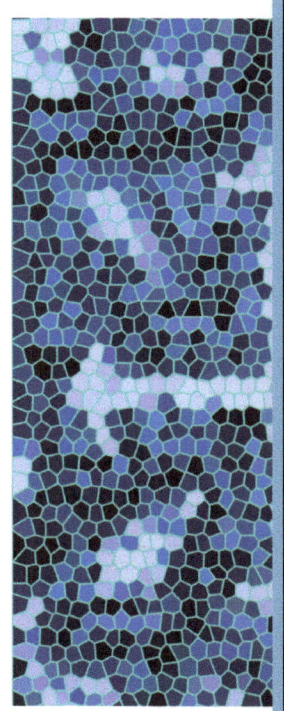
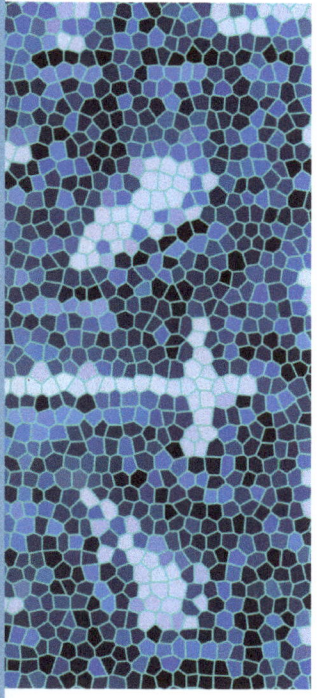

> THIS WAY OF OBEDIENCE
> UNTO DEATH
> SO THAT GOD
> MIGHT ENTER HIS STORY
> AND RAISE HIM FROM DEATH
> MUST BE THE MEASURE
> OF THE LIFE
> OF ALL WHO CLAIM
> TO BE
> HIS FOLLOWERS.

Susan Daily

who dies asking God why he has forsaken him (15:34). This portrait challenges all who follow the Son of God. He responds to his Father through his unconditional self-gift, cost him what it may (see 14:36). His followers are asked to do the same (see Mark 8:34–38).

Mark faced a problem stated by Paul some twenty years before the Gospel appeared: 'For Jews demand signs and Greeks seek wisdom, but we preach Christ crucified, a stumbling block to Jews and folly to Gentiles, but to those who are called, both Jews and Greeks, Christ the power of God and the wisdom of God. For the foolishness of God is wiser than human wisdom, and the weakness of God is stronger than any human strength' (1 Cor 1:22–25).

DID YOU KNOW

△ Mark, like Paul, wanted to teach about the meaning of Jesus' crucifixion?
△ Jesus died an agonising death, as is reported in Mark?

THE CENTREPIECE OF MARK'S GOSPEL (MARK 8:22–9:7)

The Gospel reaches its mid-point at Mark 8:30, but across 8:22–9:7 the story of Jesus tells the central message of this Gospel. On Jesus' arrival at Bethsaida, a blind man is led to him. He leads the blind man out of the village, makes spittle and puts it on his eyes, and asks him if he can see. The man receives sight, but it is an imperfect sight: men look like walking trees (8:24). He has only partially recovered his vision. In a second moment, Jesus lays his hands upon the man, and total sight is restored. He sees clearly (8:22–26). The blind man has gone from blindness (v 22) to partial sight (v 24) to a fullness of sight (v 25).

This journey of sight, from no faith to the fullness of faith, returns in the episode that follows, in the confession of Peter at Caesarea Philippi (vv 27–29). The disciples journey with Jesus to Caesarea Philippi and on the way Jesus asks them: 'Who do men say that I am?' They respond that most people think he is one of the expected messianic precursor figures: John the Baptist, Elijah or one of the prophets. He turns to his followers and asks: 'But who do you say that I am?' and Peter confesses: 'You are the Christ.' This passage has rightly been regarded as a central moment in the Gospel of Mark. For the first time in the story, someone confesses that Jesus is the Christ (see 1:1).

The confession is followed by a command from Jesus, insisting that the disciples say nothing about this to anyone (8:30).

Jesus heals a blind man

He immediately begins to teach them that the Son of Man must go to Jerusalem, suffer, and be rejected and slain by the elders, the chief priests and the scribes (v 31). Only now, in Jesus' further spelling out of what it means for him to be the Messiah, have we come to a fullness of sight. Jesus' own words reveal his true identity. The disciples' false messianic hope is already made clear in Peter's response to Jesus' self-identification as a suffering, dying and rising Son of Man. He refuses to accept that Jesus should face such a destiny, but Jesus tells him to take his correct place where all disciples should be: behind him, following him down *his* way.

The discourse that follows (8:34–9:1) enlarges upon what has happened in Jesus' command to Peter to take up his correct place as a disciple following Jesus. It is addressed to all his disciples, and to the crowd (v 34). If they wish to be followers of Jesus, his disciples, they must take up their cross and follow him. They must be prepared to tread the same path as he trod and in this way eventually come to the glory of the resurrection, also with Jesus (see v 38; 9:1). Is it possible that the Christ must suffer and die? What is more incredible is that he asks all who wish to be his disciples to follow him down this same path, if they wish to join him in his glory (8:34–9:1). Who is this man who has called them into this way of suffering and death?

The answer is found immediately in the account of the transfiguration from the Gospel of Mark (9:2–7). It presents Jesus, in the company of two figures who had ascended to heaven, as a heavenly figure. What really

34

> MARK USES THE TRADITION TO INSTRUCT HIS AUDIENCE THAT JESUS, THE ONE WHO HAS CALLED THEM INTO A LIFE OF SELF-GIFT, SUFFERING AND DEATH, IS THE SON OF GOD. THIS ALONE IS SUFFICIENT REASON FOR HIS AUDIENCE TO LISTEN TO HIM.

Susan Daily

matters, however, is the voice from heaven that explains this heavenly appearance: 'This is my beloved Son; listen to him' (v 7).

What Mark has proclaimed through the narrative made up of the series of events found side by side in Mark 8:22–9:7 can only make sense in the light of the transfiguration. It is absurd to ask followers to commit themselves to death, in the light of a promise that such commitment is life-giving (8:35). Only because of the authoritative words of God, the voice that comes from heaven, does it make sense. The readers must pay attention to the story they are hearing; they must listen: 'This is my beloved Son; listen to him!' (v 7). Mark uses the tradition to instruct his readers that Jesus, the one who has called them to follow him into a life of self-gift, suffering and death (8:34–9:1), is the Son of God. This alone is sufficient reason for all readers to 'listen to him' (9:7).

DID YOU KNOW

- △ for Mark, Jesus is the Messiah and the Son of God because of his obedient suffering and dying?
- △ according to Jesus' words, those who want to follow him must also be prepared to 'take up their cross'?
- △ many Christians over the centuries have lived the way of the cross and continue to do so?

The Gospel of Matthew

Matthew's Gospel contains three quarters of the Gospel of Mark, and much of the story-line of Matthew's life of Jesus in Mark is found again in Matthew. It was written some time in the 80s of the first century. As in Mark, and in much the same way as Mark, Jesus is the Christ, Son of God and the Son of Man (see especially Matt 16:13–16). However, Matthew, written for a Jewish–Christian community some fifteen to twenty years later than Mark develops further important teachings about Jesus and, in doing so, both *rewrites* sections of Mark's Gospel and *adds* further teaching and episodes that are not found in Mark. Matthew goes to great pains to show that Jesus does not abolish the old Law. Rather, Jesus perfects the Law, not only in what he does, but also in who he is.

There are two major additions that Matthew has made to Mark. In the first place, he reports the birth and infancy of Jesus (chapters 1–2). We will look at the infancy stories later. For Matthew, the story of Jesus' beginnings builds a bridge between God's former covenant with his chosen people, Israel, and the life of Jesus. Jesus is the fulfilment of the promises of old. Almost every scene in the infancy narrative from the Gospel of Matthew indicates that the events of Jesus' birth and infancy are 'to fulfil what was said by the prophet ...' (see 1:22–23; 2:5-6, 15, 17–18, 23). The same theme also flows into the ministry of Jesus (see 3:3; 4:6–7, 14–16). Matthew was convinced that Jesus was the

Susan Daily

perfection of all the promises of the Old Testament.

The Gospel of Matthew begins in the Old Testament, through the genealogy of Jesus (1:1–17) where God's providential handling of the history of a chosen people is already obvious. Nevertheless, the promise of the Old Testament is fulfilled in the events of the birth and the public life of Jesus.

Matthew presents the life and ministry of Jesus as the perfection of the Law. He himself attempts to live the Law perfectly and he exhorts his followers to do the same. This exhortation is found in the second major feature of Matthew: five lengthy discourses during which Jesus instructs how a 'new people of God' founded on a new and perfect Moses (see 5:1–2) should live. The five discourses match the five books of the Law: 5:1–7:28 (the sermon on the mount), 10:1–11:1 (a discourse on the future mission of the community), 13:1–53 (teaching the new people of God by parable), 18:1–35 (a discourse on the future life and order of the new people of God) and 24:1–25:45 (a discourse on the end of time and the final judgment).

The argument of Matthew's Gospel is consequently more complex than the simple twofold division of Mark. But Mark's basic story-line is evident. Matthew 'unpacks' further dimensions of that story. He tells it in the following fashion:

1:1–4:16 The coming of the Messiah

4:17–11:1 The Messiah's ministry of preaching, teaching and healing in Israel

11:2–16:12 The crisis in the Messiah's ministry

16:13–20:34 The Messiah's journey to Jerusalem

20:1–28:15 The Messiah's death and resurrection

28:16–20 The Messiah commissions his disciples

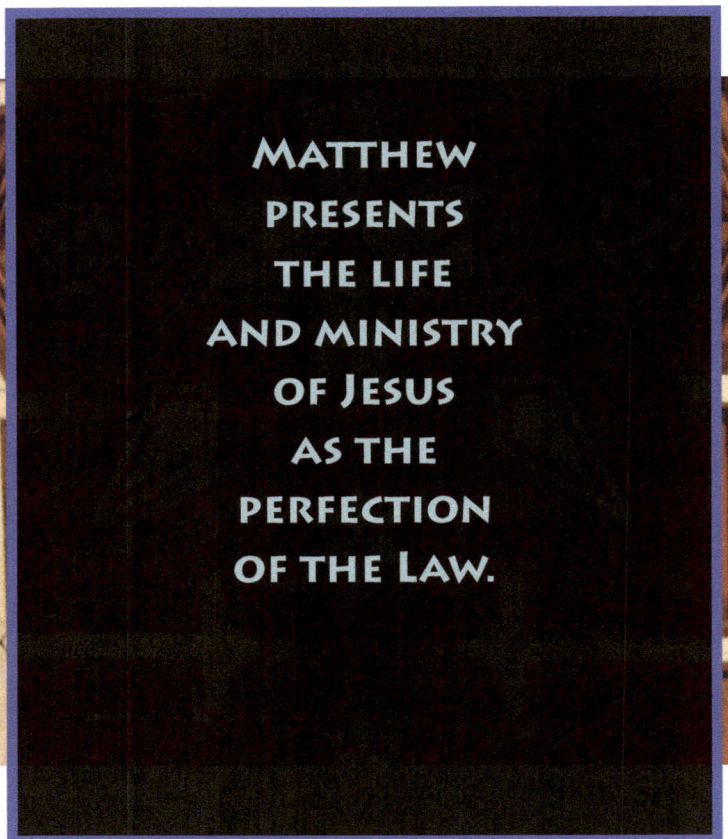

> MATTHEW PRESENTS THE LIFE AND MINISTRY OF JESUS AS THE PERFECTION OF THE LAW.

Susan Daily

During his ministry, Jesus insisted that he has come to change not an iota or a dot from the Law and the Prophets (5:17-18). He and his disciples were sent only to 'the lost sheep of Israel' (see 10:5-6; 15:24) in order to live the Law and the Prophets perfectly. But at the end of the Gospel a different message is heard. In Jesus' appearance after his death and resurrection his followers are instructed to reach beyond the perfect living of God's design for Israel and reach out to a Gentile mission – to the ends of the earth (28:16-20).

Jesus is not only the perfection of all that was promised in and through Moses. The members of Matthew's Church are sent out by a new Lord, Jesus, to whom all authority in heaven and earth has been given. Caught up in the Gentile mission, they are to teach what Jesus taught, and he will be with them till the end of all time (see 28:16-20).

Jesus fulfils the hopes of Israel as the Son of David and reaches out to all nations as the Son of Abraham (see 1:1). From his vantage point, Matthew's Jesus looks back to the past and into the future, and the person who tells the story describes himself as a scribe 'who brings out of his treasure things both new and old' (13:52).

DID YOU KNOW

△ Matthew is very interested in the Christian community as the perfect fulfilment of God's plans?
△ for Matthew, the Christian Church continues the promises made to Israel?

The universal mission of the disciples (Matthew 28:16-20)

After the Easter events (see Matt 28:1-15), the disciples return to Galilee, to the mountain indicated by Jesus (v 16). Events on a mountain recall Sinai (see Exod 19; Matt 5:1; 17:1). We are about to witness a significant communication of God's ways and teaching to the disciples. The reaction of the disciples to the sight of Jesus is ambiguous. Some worship him. Despite the fact that some of the disciples worship Jesus, and despite the climactic significance of this final scene, Matthew still reports: 'but some doubted' (v 17). All the Gospels have a realistic understanding and presentation of the disciples of Jesus. They believe, yet they falter in their belief.

The man whom they had known as Jesus of Nazareth claims that all authority on heaven and earth has been given to him (v 18). This is nothing less than to claim that Jesus has taken over the authority and dignity that traditional Israel allowed only to YHWH, the unique and traditional God of Israel. On a mountain with his hesitant disciples, Jesus claims to have been given all the authority that, according to traditional Judaism, belonged to YHWH alone. This is a bold claim. It would not have been well received by the Jews of the 80s of the first century. After the destruction of the Temple-city Jerusalem and Israel as a political entity in AD 70, Judaism had to struggle through a period of religious reconstruction. The Jews no longer had a capital city with its Temple; they no longer had a Land. Judaism gradually established its identity after the disastrous effects of the Jewish war of AD 70. A universal (although still varied) approach to YHWH was developed from the earlier Pharisaic form of pre-war Judaism. Over against the synagogue's attempts to re-establish YHWH and his Law at the centre of post-war Judaism, this Gospel presents Jesus as having been given the authority and privilege allowed only to YHWH.

Flowing from the uniqueness and universality of his authority, the Matthean Jesus then breaks

The sermon on the mount

through four further elements basic to post-AD 70 Jewish belief and practice.

1. He commands his disciples to 'Go therefore and make disciples of all nations' (v 19a). This is in direct opposition to the belief in Israel's exclusive place among the nations of the world as God's chosen people. Although there had been openness to the idea of a universal salvation with the prophets (see, for example, Isaiah 2:1–4), it had always meant a movement from the Gentile world towards Sion. Here this is reversed: the new people of God, founded by Jesus of Nazareth, are to 'go out' to make disciples of all nations.

2. The disciples are further instructed to baptise in the name of the Father and of the Son and of the Holy Spirit (v 19b), thus introducing a new initiation rite for the new people of God, setting out on their mission. It is to replace the centrally important Jewish rite of circumcision. The Christian missionary is told to replace the initiation of circumcision with baptism.

3. As if what had been commanded so far was not enough, the final command demolishes the very basis of traditional Jewish faith, built upon the teaching and the learning of the Torah. But even the Torah is replaced. Jesus uses words commonly found in passages on the importance of the Torah: 'to teach', 'to observe', 'commandments' (see, for example, Deut 5–6, especially 6:1, where all these terms appear) to indicate a new teaching: 'teaching them to observe all that I have commanded you' (v 20a). No longer does the command to teach and observe look to the Torah, but to the commandments of Jesus. The Law of Moses has been replaced by the teaching of Jesus.

4. Jesus' final words are not words of departure, but words assuring that he will always be with his disciples (v 20b). The abiding presence of Jesus will never leave his community of disciples. God has established and will sustain a holy people in and through the death and resurrection of Jesus.

Earlier in the Gospel Jesus taught that heaven and earth would have to pass away before the Law and the prophets could be perfected (5:17–18). This has happened in Jesus' death (see 27:45, 51–53) and resurrection (28:2–3). The end of Matthew's Gospel shows that Jesus' mission and the mission of the disciples can no longer be limited to 'the lost sheep of Israel'. Jesus' death and resurrection mark a turning point in God's relationship with humankind. We are now sent out on a journey into a world of universal mission, confident in the abiding presence of Jesus, but always remembering where we came from, bringing out of our treasures 'things both new and old' (13:52).

DID YOU KNOW

△ Matthew is more interested in Peter than any of the other Gospels are?

△ in Matthew's Gospel Jesus founds the Church and its teaching authority on Peter?

The Gospel of Luke

Although one of the 'synoptic' Gospels (along with Mark and Matthew), there is a lot that is different about the Gospel of Luke, also written (like Matthew) some time in the 80s of the first century. *Only Luke* portrays the image of Mary, the mother of Jesus, in the fashion that Christians have come to love and accept. There are many narratives and parables found *only in Luke:* the restoration of the only son to a widow at Nain (Luke 7:11-17), John the Baptist, still wondering if Jesus is the one who is to come (7:18-23), the shock generated by Jesus' attention to, and forgiveness of, a sinful woman who enters the house of a Pharisee to perform an erotic ritual (7:36-50), the scandal of the women who go on a journey with this itinerant preacher (8:1-3), the good Samaritan (10:25-37), Martha and Mary (10:38-42), the parable of the great banquet (14:15-25), the parable of the lost sheep (15:3-7), the parable of the lost coin (15:8-10), the parable of the father with two lost sons (15:11-32), the parable of the cunning steward (16:1-9), the rich man and Lazarus (16:19-31), the one cured leper – a Samaritan – who returns to thank Jesus (17:11-19), the parable of the Pharisee and the tax collector (18:9-14), Jesus and Zacchaeus (19:1-10), and Jesus' weeping over Jerusalem (19:41-44).

In the story of the passion Jesus' final words of despair in Matthew and Mark ('My God, my God, why have your forsaken me?' [Mark 15:34; Matt 27:46]), become: 'Father, forgive them, for they know not what they do' (23:35), 'Truly, I say to you, today you will be with me in Paradise' (23:43), 'Father, into your hands I commend my spirit' (23:46). The Roman centurion does not say: 'Truly this man was the Son of God' (Mark 15:39; Matt 27:54), but he praises God, exclaiming, 'Certainly this man was innocent' (Luke 23:47). The resurrection is highlighted by the story of the journey to Emmaus (24:13-35) and Jesus' commission as Risen Lord: 'Thus it is written, that the Christ should suffer and on the third day rise from the dead, and that repentance and forgiveness should be preached in his name to all the nations, beginning in Jerusalem. You are witnesses of these things. And behold, I send the promise of my Father upon you; but stay in the city, until you have been clothed with power from on high' (24:46-49).

Despite the large amount of material that comes only from Luke and his traditions, and despite this author's outstanding storytelling ability found in the details of this Gospel, it unfolds in a way that continues to recall the simple design of the first Gospel, Mark. Luke's story unfolds as follows:

1:1-4 Dedication to Theophilus
1:5-4:13 The coming of the Messiah, Son of God
4:14-9:50 Jesus' ministry in Galilee

9:51–19:44 Jesus and his disciples' journey to Jerusalem. This section is different from the other Gospels

19:45–21:38 Jesus in Jerusalem

22:1–24:53 Jesus' passion, death, resurrection and ascension.

Notice that the most unique feature of the overall structure of this Gospel is the long journey that Jesus makes with his disciples to Jerusalem (9:51–19:44). Much of the material that is found only in Luke appears here. The theme of 'journey' appears important to Luke. In Luke's ongoing story (the Acts of the Apostles) the apostles do as they were commanded. They stay in the city. After forty days, as Jesus ascends, he again instructs them: 'You shall receive power when the Holy Spirit has come upon you; and you shall be my witnesses in Jerusalem and in all Judea and Samaria and to the end of the earth' (Acts 1:8). The story that follows tells of the gift of the Holy Spirit (2:1–4), the community in Jerusalem (2:5–8:1), the mission into Judea and Samaria (8:2–13:7), and by means of Paul's journeys, a journey to the ends of the earth. As the second volume of Luke's work comes to a close, indeed, in its very last line, Paul is in Rome 'preaching the kingdom of God and teaching about the Lord Jesus Christ quite openly and unhindered' (28:31).

> **LUKE TELLS THE STORY OF THE BIRTH, LIFE AND TEACHING, DEATH, RESURRECTION AND ASCENSION OF JESUS, FOLLOWED BY THE JOURNEY OF THE EARLIEST CHURCH TO THE ENDS OF THE EARTH.**

Luke tells the story of the birth, life and teaching, death, and resurrection and ascension of Jesus, followed by the journey of the earliest Church to the ends of the earth (see Luke 24:47; Acts 1:8). It could be said that contemporary readers of the Gospel of Luke and the Acts of the Apostles are part of the as yet unfinished third volume. That story will be told until the end of time. As the two men in white robes say to the first disciples who stand gazing into the sky after Jesus' ascension: 'Men of Galilee, why do you stand looking into heaven? This Jesus, who was taken up from you into heaven, will come back in the same way as you saw him go into heaven' (Acts 1:10–11). During the time of the Church, the 'in-between-time', there is a job to be done. Why are you standing motionless, looking into the clouds?

Luke continues the tradition initiated by Mark and continued by Matthew. Jesus is the Christ, the Son of God, and the suffering and risen Son of Man who will come as judge. However, this overview of the elements in Luke's Gospel that are *unique to Luke* show that Luke wants to teach something further about Jesus: he is the Lord of all history.

DID YOU KNOW

△ Luke is more interested in Mary, the mother of Jesus, than any of the other Gospels are?

△ Luke has kept most of Jesus' well-loved parables?

THE PARABLE OF LIMITLESS COMPASSION (LUKE 15:1–32)

Let us listen to and reflect upon some Lucan parables (from the Gospel of Luke). Tax collectors and sinners are drawing near to hear Jesus. The Pharisees and the scribes exclaim: 'This man receives sinners and eats with them' (15:1–2).

Two brief parables, constructed very similarly, and a further lengthy parable are found in Luke 15. The brief parables ask the question that will be answered in the parable of the father with two sons. Jesus asks seriously: which one of you, if you had a hundred sheep, would leave ninety-nine of them in the wilderness and go in search of the one that was lost? (v 4). The answer to that question is easy: no one would do such a silly thing. But the search to bring the sinner to repentance goes to crazy lengths and leads to great rejoicing when that which was lost is found (vv 5–7). Similarly, which woman, having ten coins, would turn her home upside down simply to find one that was lost? As with the lost sheep, the finding of the lost coin leads to great rejoicing. What was lost is found (vv 8–10).

The parable of the father with the two sons stretches the message to the limit. He sets his younger son free so that he can make his own choices and bear their consequences (vv 12–16). He is waiting for the son as he returns, and welcomes him back into the household with great joy and celebration (vv 17–24). The real point of the parable, however, is found in its conclusion. This father runs the risk of losing his older son. One of them was lost and has been found, but as

Madonna and Child Mosaic, Church of the Visitation, Ein Karem, Israel Susan Daily

the parable comes to a close, the father is outside, away from the rejoicing, trying to save his second lost son, to whom he says: 'My son, you are always with me. Everything I have is yours' (v 31). This may be read simply as the economic consequence of the younger son having squandered his half of the family inheritance. But that would be a superficial interpretation. Jesus points to a father who makes serious demands of all who would be his followers (see 9:51–14:35), but these demands must now be read in the bright light of a father who will always be found in unexpected places, searching for his lost sons and daughters (vv 25–32). What is lost must be found (see v 32; see also 5:31–32). This is the message that stands at the centre of a major section of Luke's presentation of Jesus: his journey to Jerusalem (9:51–19:44).

In the Gospel of Luke as a whole story, Jesus not only tells this parable, he lives it. As Luke tells Jesus' story, the crucified Jesus is abused: 'He saved others, let him save himself' (23:35), and Jesus' first words to the people in Nazareth return to the reader: 'Doubtless you will quote me this proverb, "Physician, heal yourself"' (4:23). Jesus has been rendered powerless by his decision to love without condition. Nailed securely on solid wood he is powerless. For Luke, however, he lives out the parable in unconditional love. His last words forgive all who have rejected him (see 23:34). He invites them, in the person of the thief on the cross, to join him in the banquet prepared for all his lost sons and daughters in paradise (see 23:39–43). It is Jesus who has *told* and *lived* a parable of the powerless almighty God, his and our Father. Jesus knows his Father

> **THE GOD REVEALED BY JESUS IS AS MUCH A SURPRISE TO US TODAY AS IT WAS TO JESUS' ORIGINAL LISTENERS AND LUKE'S ORIGINAL READERS.**

Susan Daily

in heaven better than anyone else knows him (see 10:21–22). Should it not be true that this Father in heaven is to be found, first of all, where the father stands at the end of the parable – outside, away from the rejoicing, seeking his second lost son?

A proper understanding of Luke's use of this parable raises at least two concerns.

He revealed a different sort of God than the one expected and invented by the religions and culture of his own day. The message retains its power today, because we continue to look for God in the wrong places. The God revealed by Jesus is as much a surprise to us today as it was to Jesus' original listeners and Luke's original readers. He can be found out in the dark, trying to save his lost children.

Jesus of Nazareth 'lived' the parable; he did not just 'tell' it. Jesus was and is the parable of God. In a unique way, therefore, Jesus reveals God's presence in everything he says and does. The image of limitless compassion, as a manifestation of limitless love, is a challenging proclamation of a God that we must seek out in the most unexpected places.

DID YOU KNOW

△ the parable of the prodigal son is really about the Father?
△ the message of the parable is still very challenging?

The Birth Stories in Matthew 1–2 and Luke 1–2

The Nativity

Before leaving the synoptic Gospels, let us look at the stories of Jesus' birth and infancy, as told in the Gospel of Matthew (chapters 1-2) and the Gospel of Luke (chapters 1-2). Only these two Gospels have so-called birth stories.

The celebration of Christmas, and the symbols we use during that celebration, nearly all come from the Gospel of Luke. Similarly, the Joyful Decades of the Rosary in the Catholic tradition all come from the Gospel of Luke: the Annunciation (Luke 1:26–38), the Visitation (1:39–56), the Birth of Jesus (2:1–24), the Presentation of the Child Jesus in the Temple (2:25–40), and the Finding of the Child Jesus in the Temple (2:41–52). These are joy and faith-filled stories of wonderful women (Elizabeth and Mary), John the Baptist, shepherds, angels, Simeon, Anna and the child Jesus among the wise men in the Temple. The dominant character is Mary, the mother of Jesus, who hears the Word of God and does it.

The only episode from the Gospel of Matthew that creeps into the Christmas celebrations is the shadowy account of the slaying of the Innocents (Matt 2:16–18). The joyful proclamation of the Lucan story is absent as Matthew tells Jesus' genealogy (1:1–17), the suspicion of an illegitimate child to be born of Mary (1:18–25), the visit of the Magi while Herod plots (2:1–12), the flight into Egypt (2:13–15), the slaying of the Innocents (2:16–18), the return of Joseph and his family from Egypt only to flee again from Judea to Nazareth in Galilee (2:19–23). The dominant character is Joseph, the supposed father of Jesus, who also hears the Word of God and does it.

As with everything in the Gospels, each author has told the story in different ways. No doubt there were popular stories that Luke knew, and that is what appears in his account, while Matthew also used familiar stories. Matthew and Luke told their stories in different ways for at least two reasons: to

46

serve as an introduction to the person of Jesus to their different readers/listeners and to serve as a prologue to the whole story. In other words, you can only understand Luke's portrait of Jesus properly, and Matthew's portrait of Jesus properly, if you have understood what we are told about him in the birth and infancy stories. Once you understand who Jesus is, and where he comes from (Matt 1–2 and Luke 1–2), then you are ready to read the story of his ministry, his teaching, his death and his resurrection. Matthew's story of Jesus is different from that of Luke's and this is reflected in their different birth and infancy stories.

But are we able to find anything behind these different stories that may go back to the events that surrounded Jesus' birth? Indeed we are. Both stories tell of Mary and Joseph, Jesus' mother and his supposed father. Both locate Jesus' birth about the time of the end of the reign of Herod the Great (4 BC). Both stories (although in different ways) tell that Jesus' conception is the result of the action of God and not of the union between Mary and Joseph. Both stories locate the place where Jesus grew up as Nazareth, even though he is born in the city of David and Joseph is of the line of David. Thus, for both accounts, Jesus is understood as being from the Davidic line. Behind the two different stories there is something they share which cannot be explained: Jesus is from God.

There are two moments in Jesus' human experience that are beyond human measurement and understanding: how he came into the world (virgin birth) and how he went out of it (resurrection and ascension). Jesus embraces the human condition without reservation. But the Gospels leave his origins and his destiny in the mystery of his being one with God. It is here that the New Testament summons its readers to abandon all attempts to 'control and measure' the person of Jesus, and recognise that we are being blessed by God's action among us and for us. 'She will bear a son, and you are to name him Jesus, for he will save his people from their sins' (Matt 1:21).

Angel Gabriel (after Fra Angelico) Lynne Muir

DID YOU KNOW

△ the stories of Jesus' birth and infancy in Matthew and Luke were so different?

△ both stories teach us so much about Jesus' identity and mission?

The Gospel of John

The Gospel of John is a much-loved Christian document. Many of its passages 'ring a bell' with any Christian. No scholarly training is needed for us to be moved by the proclamation 'The Word became flesh and lived among us, and we have seen his glory, the glory as of the Father's only son, the fullness of a gift which is truth' (John 1:14). We share the belief expressed by the Samaritan villagers: 'We know that this is truly the Savior of the world' (4:42), by Martha: 'Lord, I believe that you are the Messiah, the Son of God, the one coming into the world', and Thomas: 'My Lord and my God' (20:28). We respond with joy to Jesus' promises: 'You will know the truth, and the truth will set you free' (8:32), 'I am the way, the truth and the life' (14:6). But this Gospel was not written as a collection of inspiring and comforting words. On the contrary, it came into existence to create *crisis*, not *comfort*.

The Gospel of John, at first sight, is relatively simple to divide into a Prologue, two major sections and a conclusion. The Prologue (John 1:1–18) is one of the most remarkable passages in the New Testament, and it stands alone, introducing the story of the life and teaching of Jesus. Before entering the day-to-day telling of the life and ministry of Jesus, the reader knows that the Logos existed before all time, in intimate union with God. As such, the Logos made God known, but came among his own and was refused. But those who accepted him could become his children. The Logos became flesh and his name was Jesus Christ. We have seen him, and in him we have had God made known to us.

The raising of Lazarus

With the information in our minds and hearts, we begin to read a narrative about Jesus' public ministry. We first read of John the Baptist's activity (1:19–34), but once Jesus enters the scene, he calls his disciples and becomes the main focus of attention. He journeys with his disciples, from one miracle at Cana (2:1–12) to another (4:46–54), summoning various people to true faith. He then journeys to and from Jerusalem for the feasts of Israel: Sabbath (5:1–47; 6:1–72), Tabernacles (7:1–10:21) and Dedication (10:22–42). Across these feasts he presents himself as the sent one by the Father who embodies the central celebration of the feasts: lord of all (Sabbath), bread from heaven (Passover), living water, the light of the world and the Messiah (Tabernacles) and the living presence of God in Jerusalem (Dedication).

The raising of Lazarus (11:1–54) is not really about sickness, but about life, and through this miracle Jesus begins his journey to the cross, the revelation of the glory of God and the means by which Jesus will be glorified (see v 4). The decision is made that he must die, not only for the nation, but to gather into one the children of God who are scattered abroad (11:49–53). Jesus enters Jerusalem, the Greeks seek him and the hour of his glorification has come – his lifting up, his drawing everyone to himself on his cross (12:1–36)!

Jesus' last night with the disciples is very different from the synoptic Gospels. He washes their feet and shares bread with them, despite their failure, because he loved them to the very end (13:1–38; 17:1–26). He tells them he must leave them, but he will not

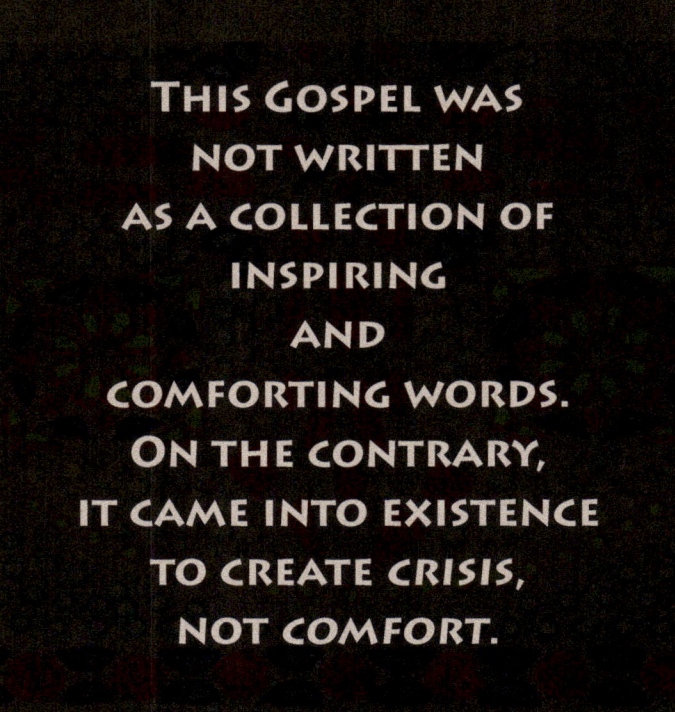

> THIS GOSPEL WAS NOT WRITTEN AS A COLLECTION OF INSPIRING AND COMFORTING WORDS. ON THE CONTRARY, IT CAME INTO EXISTENCE TO CREATE CRISIS, NOT COMFORT.

Susan Daily

abandon them. They will be given the Spirit Paraclete (14:1–31; 16:4–33) and they must live according to Jesus' commandments of faith and love in the midst of hatred and persecution (15:1–16:3).

John's story of Jesus' passion repeats the story told in the synoptic Gospels – the Garden of Olives (18:1–11), Jewish hearing (18:12–27), Roman trial (18:28–19:16a), death and crucifixion (19:16b–37), and burial (19:38–42) – but it is told differently. Jesus is in control at all times. He is crowned and proclaimed as a king by Pilate, and he is crucified as a king, despite being rejected by those who will not accept this revelation of God's love for us. Similarly, while the events of the resurrection are the same – empty tomb, and Mary Magdalene; appearances and a commission to his disciples – the story is different. Mary Magdalene, the Beloved Disciple, the disciples and Thomas all come to true faith in Jesus.

However, this story is written for us also. Jesus blesses those who believe without seeing (20:29). John tells us he wrote this Gospel so that we might come to believe and have life (20:30–31). A further chapter (John 21), added after the author had penned 20:30–31, has always been part of this story of Jesus. More was to be said to the disciples, and all subsequent disciples who might read this Gospel: the universal mission of the Church (21:1–14), the authority of Peter the shepherd (vv 15–19) and the witness of the Beloved Disciple (vv 20–24) must be affirmed before the book can be closed (v 25).

DID YOU KNOW

△ the Gospel of John was so different from the other Gospels?
△ much of the Christian understanding of Jesus comes from John?

Loving to the very end (John 13:1–38)

Jesus knows the hour has come for his return to the Father. He has brought to perfection the work his Father gave him to do (see 4:34). Having loved his own on earth, he is aware that the hour has come for him to return to the Father. Without further ado, however, something dramatically new is introduced. We are told the moment of 'completion' has arrived in a love that is both the final act in a human story and a gesture of love which cannot be surpassed: 'he loved them to the very end'. The expression 'to the very end' has two meanings. It means a point in time, to the end of his life on the cross. It also tells of the quality of his wonderful and immeasurable love. Jesus' departure from this world to the Father, in a consummate act of love for 'his own', will be *via* the Cross.

In the Gospel's report of the final moments of Jesus' public ministry with his disciples and among the crowds of people who both accept him, reject him, or remain indifferent, Jesus has already set the agenda for what is now about to be explained by Jesus' deeds and words. As the Greeks arrived, the hour of the glorification of the Son of Man was announced (12:23) and explained as a 'lifting up' (12:32–33).

The disciples are swept up into Jesus' love by means of two gestures. In the first, Jesus adopts the position of the most menial servant or slave. He takes off his clothes and washes the feet of the disciples. This remarkable gesture of his love for them 'to the very end' is met only with rumblings of Judas' future betrayal (vv 2, 10–11), Peter's inability to understand what Jesus is doing for them (vv 6–9), and the general ignorance of the other disciples (v 12). Despite

Susan Daily

their failure, ignorance, denial and betrayal, they belong to Jesus, and thus are promised the blessings that will flow from his death and resurrection, events that are foreshadowed in the symbolic footwashing (see v 8), and he challenges them to be his disciples by accepting the new example he has shown them: as he has done for them, so they must do for one another (v 15).

Why is he doing this for them, showing how much he loves them in the midst of their betrayal, ignorance and failure? He tells them in verse 19: 'I tell you this now before it occurs, so that when it does occur you may believe that I AM HE.' What he is doing and saying – loving them to the end, and asking them to love in the same way – is leading them into belief in him as the revelation of the love of God (I AM HE).

In the second half of the chapter, another loving gesture is seen in the gift of the morsel (vv 21–28). Again, this symbolic gesture of Jesus' love for his own takes place in the shadow of Judas' betrayal (vv 21–28), Peter's denials (vv 36–38) and the ignorance of all the disciples (vv 28–29). As Judas leaves the room to go into the darkness of the night, the same theme returns. The Son of Man is now glorified and God is glorified in him (vv 30–32). Just as he had used the symbol of the 'foot-washing' as an example of his never-ending love, and had asked the disciples to follow this example, he now makes the same request after the gift of the Eucharistic morsel. He tells them: 'I give you a new commandment that you love one another, just as I have loved you, you also should love one another. By this everyone will know that you are my disciples, if you have love for one another' (vv 34–35).

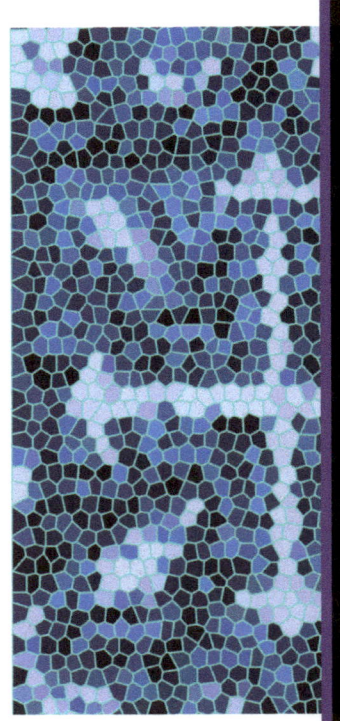
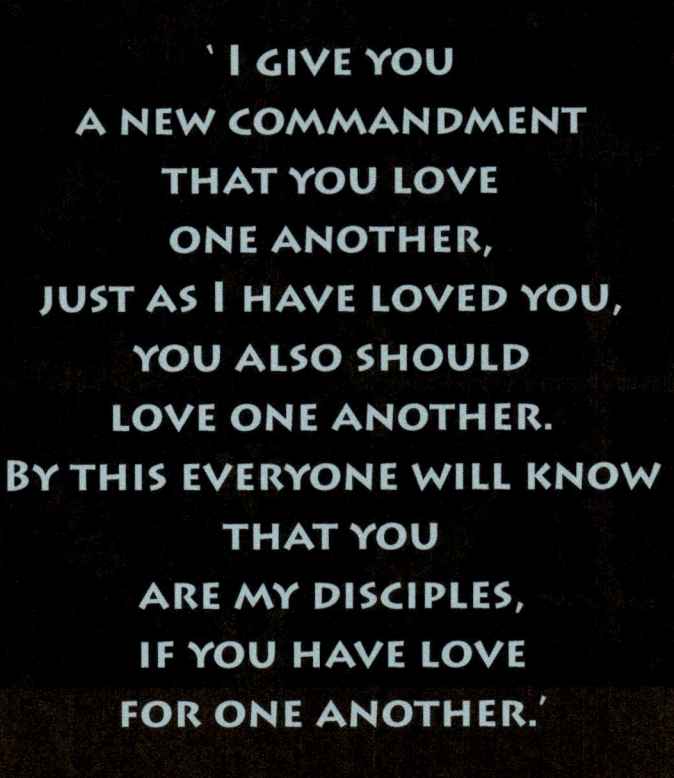
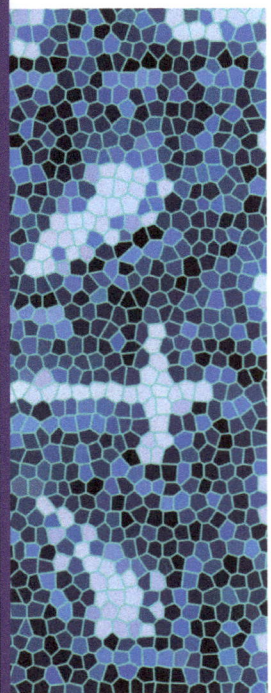

'I GIVE YOU A NEW COMMANDMENT THAT YOU LOVE ONE ANOTHER, JUST AS I HAVE LOVED YOU, YOU ALSO SHOULD LOVE ONE ANOTHER. BY THIS EVERYONE WILL KNOW THAT YOU ARE MY DISCIPLES, IF YOU HAVE LOVE FOR ONE ANOTHER.'

Susan Daily

The stage is being set for Jesus' lifting up on the cross, so that all can gaze upon the pierced one, and see in him the revelation of God's love (see 19:37). Later in the final discourse that Jesus has with his disciples he explains why his death tells us how much he loves us: 'No one has greater love than this, to lay down one's life for one's friends. You are my friends if you do what I command you' (15:13–14).

The love which is to be revealed in Jesus' self-gift will be continued in the lives of 'his own', whom he leaves in the world (13:12–17, 33–35). Jesus tells these things to fragile disciples, whom he has chosen and will send out, so that when this moment of glorification takes place, they might believe that Jesus is the revelation of God: 'so that you might believe that I am he' (v 19). Jesus makes God known in the perfect love he shows for his fragile disciples. In and through his loving, Jesus is glorified, and God is glorified in him. The disciples are to be recognised as the sent ones of Jesus by the unity created in the love they have for one another.

DID YOU KNOW

△ John tells us so much about the greatness of God's love shown to us in Jesus?

△ Baptism and the Eucharist were so important in the earliest Church?

Saint Paul

The power of the resurrection

Paul was a Jew 'of the people of Israel, of the tribe of Benjamin, a Hebrew born of Hebrews' (Phil 3:5). He also tells us that he belonged to the Jewish sect of the Pharisees (Phil 3:5). Luke informs us that Paul was educated to his Pharisaism in Jerusalem by Gamaliel (Acts 22:3), the Rabbi made famous in Christian tradition for his wise advice about allowing the new Christian movement to run free, either to failure if it were a mere human creation, or to flourish if it were of God (Acts 5:35–39). Paul himself tells us nothing of that background. He regularly admits that his passion for the Law and its observance led him to a 'zeal' that could not tolerate the emerging form of sectarian Judaism which claimed that the crucified Jesus of Nazareth was the Christ (Phil 3:6; Gal 1:13, 23; 1 Cor 15:9). That all changed.

Paul was transformed by what we might nowadays call a 'religious experience' that turned his life around to such an extent that he spent his whole life, even to the point of martyrdom, in

Lynne Muir

a passionate gift of himself to preaching the gospel: 'Woe to me if I do not preach the gospel' (1 Cor 9:16).

In Paul's letters there is no journey to Damascus, no falling from a horse, no voice from heaven, no blindness and no mention of Straight Street and Ananias. What Paul does tell us, however, is that he experienced a 'sight' of the risen Jesus. It was this revelation that was the foundation of his call to be an apostle of Jesus Christ to the Gentiles (see 1 Cor 9:1; 15:8; Gal 1:12–16). Paul confirms that this experience took place near Damascus (Gal 1:17; 2 Cor 11:32), but the geography does not interest him. Did Paul have a 'conversion'? Maybe not. Underlying Paul's zeal as a Jew and his zeal as a Christian was a single-minded passion for the one true God that was always with him. His passion for God was not changed by means of a conversion, but he experienced a 'call' from that God to recognise and proclaim what God had done for humankind in and through his Son.

Paul tells us of his transformation in Philippians 3:7–11 (RSV) (the emphasis is the author's):

> But whatever gain I had, I counted as loss for the sake of Christ. Indeed I count

everything as loss because of the surpassing worth of knowing Christ Jesus my Lord. For his sake I have suffered the loss of all things, and count them as refuse, in order that I may gain Christ and be found in him, not having a righteousness of my own based on law, but that which is through faith in Christ, the righteousness from God that depends on faith; that I may know him and *the power of his resurrection*, and may share his sufferings, becoming like him in his death, that if possible I may attain the resurrection from the dead. (See also 1 Cor 1:18; 2 Cor 4:7; 12:9; 13:4.)

For Paul, and the gospel he preached, the only things that mattered were:

≈ To know Christ Jesus as Lord
≈ To gain Christ and to be found in him
≈ To have right relationship (righteousness) with God through belief in what God has done for us in and through Jesus Christ
≈ To reject any idea that such a relationship can be generated by anything human, such as the observance of restrictive practices associated with the Law
≈ To live and die as Jesus of Nazareth lived and died, becoming like him in suffering and death
≈ To eventually share also in Jesus' resurrection from the dead

Susan Daily

The source for Paul's relentless and passionate conviction that these were the only things that mattered, was *the power of the resurrection*.

Paul tells us little of the life of Jesus. In the fullness of time, Jesus was born of a woman (Gal 4:4); the night before he died he celebrated a meal with his disciples that looked to his suffering, death and ultimate victory through resurrection for its meaning (1 Cor 11:23–26); he was crucified, buried, raised, and seen by a multitude of witnesses (1 Cor 15: 1–8). The last of these witnesses, the one untimely and unworthily born, was Paul himself (15:8–9). At the heart of his preaching was Jesus' death and resurrection. As he tells us, in his first letter to the Corinthians:

For Jews demand signs and Greeks seek wisdom, but we preach Christ crucified, a stumbling block to Jews and folly to Gentiles, but to those who are called, both Jews and Greeks, Christ the power of God and the wisdom of God. For the foolishness of God is wiser than men, and the weakness of God is stronger than men. (1 Cor 1:22–25 RSV)

Crucifixion is transformed into power and wisdom, weakness into strength. The power and the wisdom of God are manifested in what Paul has called 'the power of the resurrection'. As we will see, it generates a 'new creation'.

DID YOU KNOW

△ Paul does not tell much of the story of Jesus as we have it in the Gospels?
△ the crucifixion is at the heart of Paul's message?

THE DEATH AND RESURRECTION OF JESUS (PHILIPPIANS 2:5–11)

Rather than reading across all Paul's letters to trace the significance of Jesus' death and resurrection, we will focus our attention on a famous Pauline 'hymn', found in Philippians 2:5–11. As you read the following analysis, be sure to follow what Paul actually says in the passage. It appears that there was division among the Philippians. Just prior to the hymn he writes: 'Do nothing from selfish ambition or conceit, but in humility regard others as better than yourselves. Let each of you look not to your own interests, but to the interests of others.' Paul immediately re-writes the hymn for them. They knew this hymn, as they sang it regularly in praise of Jesus Christ. By telling the Philippians 'Let the same mind be in you that was in Christ Jesus' (v 5), he tells them that their only model can be Jesus. The hymn they sing tells his story, but perhaps it is not telling the story of the Philippians. He asks them to put their lives where their words are.

This famous hymn unfolds in four stages. The first is brief, describing Jesus' pre-existent divine state. But it affirms that Jesus did not cling on rapaciously to the honour of being equal to God. The Greek verb used for 'cling' is a violent word, well chosen because most of us do cling jealously to our honours. Scholars have debated for decades why this rough and almost violent Greek verb (*harpazo*) could be used in a hymn dedicated to Jesus. What must be noticed is that the verb is in the negative!

This is what Jesus *did not do*: 'he *did not* regard equality with God as something to be exploited'. Paul speaks directly to us all. As we seek honours and glory in our achievements, Christ Jesus did exactly the opposite. He lets go of the most wonderful of honours – his oneness with God. His status was divine and he let it go; our status is fragile and sinful, but we 'grasp onto it jealously'.

This leads the hymn into the first step in the second stage – the first description of Christ's humiliation. Jesus does not simply

Philippians 2:5–11

⁵*Let the same mind be in you that was in Christ Jesus,*	Exhortation to the Philippians
⁶who, though he was in the form of God,	Humiliation 1
did not regard equality with God as something to be exploited,	
⁷but emptied himself,	
taking the form of a slave,	
being born in human likeness.	Humiliation 2
And being found in human form,	
⁸he humbled himself	
and became obedient to the point of death –	
even death on the cross.	
⁹Therefore God also highly exalted him	Exaltation
and gave him the name	
that is above every name,	
¹⁰so that at the name of Jesus	Homage 1
every knee should bend,	
in heaven and on earth and under the earth,	
¹¹and every tongue should confess	Homage 2
that Jesus Christ is Lord,	
to the glory of God the Father.	

'let go', he 'empties himself' of all such dignity to take on the situation of a servant and slave. He comes into the history of frail human beings as a frail human being – he became as men are. But the second description of Jesus' humiliation points out that he lowered himself in human eyes to the lowest of the low, he accepted the cruellest and most humiliating death – death on a cross. Only when Jesus gives his unconditional 'yes' to God on the Cross is his humiliation complete. This is the most perfect form of unconditional *obedience* that one could ever expect from a human being.

The hymn has had a downward swing from the pre-existent Christ, equal to God, to a human being, who was also a crucified slave. The unconditional obedience of Jesus has touched the human story in a 'once and for all' fashion and this has its consequence. Jesus' unconditional 'yes' to God is now met by an unconditional 'yes' from God.

Because of what Jesus did out of obedience to God and for all of us, he is raised on high by God. The theme of the hymn begins its upward swing with this turning

Susan Daily

point in the unfolding hymn – in the resurrection God has highly exalted him. Through the resurrection, the Christ returns to the place he abandoned so that we may have life and hope.

The result of God's exaltation of his Son does not lead the Christ to a distant place on the altars on high. Jesus' death and resurrection have changed the nature of the relationship between God and humankind.

He is given the name of Lord. All creation recognises what he has done and bends the knee in recognition of the saving act of God that has taken place through obedience unto death and the exaltation that takes place in resurrection. Jesus Christ is now our Lord and the Lord of all. We no longer have to wait for the end of all time for the establishment of God's 'right order'. It has been made present among us in the new creation in and through the obedient death, resurrection, and universal Lordship of Jesus Christ. We confess that Jesus Christ is Lord; we recognise the glory of God, but only if we are prepared to accept Paul's initial invitation to 'walk as Jesus walked': 'Let the same mind be in you that was in Christ Jesus'. The story of Jesus must be repeated in the story of all who claim to follow him. In this way our lives will be caught up into the rhythm, scope and ultimate victory of the same divine plan.

DID YOU KNOW

△ Paul asks us to be followers of Jesus, to live as Jesus lived?

△ Paul challenged his communities to not just talk about their belief, but to show it by letting the same mind be in them as was in Jesus?

The New Creation (Romans 5:12-21)

On two occasions, Paul speaks – without explanation – of the death and resurrection having generated a 'new creation' (Gal 2:15; 2 Cor 5:17). He may not use the expression itself elsewhere, but Paul's understanding of what God has done for us in the death and resurrection of Jesus is well expressed as a 'new creation'. One of the best explanations of this is found in Romans 5:12-21. Just as we looked at Philippians 2:5-11 for a concise presentation of Paul's central message on Jesus' death and resurrection, we will now read Romans 5:12-21 carefully for an understanding of what God has done for us in the new creation.

Like all Jews, Paul accepted that 'in the beginning' (Genesis 1:1) everything was exactly as God wanted it. God's glory and God's will were evident in creation and in the lives of Adam and Eve. However, sin entered the world through the disobedience of Adam, and once sin had begun, it gradually spread and took possession of the whole of God's originally perfect creation: 'Sin came into the world through one man' (v 12). Long after the universal spread of sin, the Law was given to Moses. Sin abounded. Even the Law could not free us from the slavery of sin (v 13). It could protect us, but not save us.

Saul, along with his Jewish contemporaries, believed that final salvation and the restoration of a world as God had made it would take place 'at the end' of all time. God would restore everything to its original beauty. Jewish belief was based upon the conviction that the loss of God's glory in the world because of the sin of Adam, at the beginning of all time, would be matched by the restoration of God's glory, at the end of all time. What was at the beginning, the glory of God, would be restored by God at the end.

But, as we have seen, Paul had been swept up into the power of Jesus' death and resurrection. These events took place during the course of ordinary human history – before the final end of time. Now Paul became a passionate believer that we did not have to wait till the end of time for God's way in the world to be re-established. God broke into the passage of ordinary human time in and through Jesus Christ. Jesus, taking on the sinful condition of humankind (Phil 2:7-8), reversed Adam's sin

Romans 5:12-21

¹²Therefore, just as sin came into the world through one man, and death came through sin, and so death spread to all because all have sinned– ¹³sin was indeed in the world before the law, but sin is not reckoned when there is no law. ¹⁴Yet death exercised dominion from Adam to Moses, even over those whose sins were not like the transgression of Adam, who is a type of the one who was to come. ¹⁵But the free gift is not like the trespass. For if the many died through the one man's trespass, much more surely have the grace of God and the free gift in the grace of the one man, Jesus Christ, abounded for the many. ¹⁶And the free gift is not like the effect of the one man's sin. For the judgment following one trespass brought condemnation, but the free gift following many trespasses brings justification. ¹⁷If, because of the one man's trespass, death exercised dominion through that one, much more surely will those who receive the abundance of grace and the free gift of righteousness exercise dominion in life through the one man, Jesus Christ. ¹⁸Therefore just as one man's trespass led to condemnation for all, so one man's act of righteousness leads to justification and life for all. ¹⁹For just as by the one man's disobedience the many were made sinners, so by the one man's obedience the many will be made righteous. ²⁰But law came in, with the result that the trespass multiplied; but where sin increased, grace abounded all the more, ²¹so that, just as sin exercised dominion in death, so grace might also exercise dominion through justification leading to eternal life through Jesus Christ our Lord.

of disobedience by means of his unconditional obedience to God. Because of Jesus' death and resurrection, therefore, what had been expected to happen only at the end of all time was already happening: 'Therefore, just as one man's trespass led to condemnation for all, so one man's act of righteousness leads to justification and life for all. For as by the one man's disobedience the many were made sinners, so by the one man's obedience the many will be made righteous' (Rom 5:18–19).

This adversarial relationship between the disobedience of Adam, and its consequences of sin and death, and the obedience of Jesus Christ, with its consequences of an abundance of God's free gifts, leading to right relationship with him, explains what Paul means when he describes Adam as 'a type of the one who was to come' (v 14). It is not that Jesus repeats Adam. He is only a 'type' in so far as he is an 'anti-type'. But what both Adam and Jesus Christ share is the universal effect of their contrasting responses to God. Adam's disobedience generated universal sin and death. Jesus Christ's obedience generated the possibility of universal right

Susan Daily

relationship with God.

Union with God and the fullness of life are now available. What Jesus did for us introduced a 'new creation'. The beauty of God's original creation had been disfigured by sin. It has been restored in the new creation made possible by obedience unto death and the resurrection of Jesus. What was wrecked by one man's disobedience has been restored by another man's obedience.

This message is stated over and over in the chosen passage. But we must always remember that Paul was a realist. The sinful condition established by the sin of Adam has not disappeared. The ruination of the original creation that set loose sin and death in the whole world is still abroad. It runs side by side with the grace and freedom established in the new creation made possible in Jesus Christ. We are called to choose which story we would like to join: that of Adam, or that of Jesus Christ.

The choice before us, both individually and collectively, is 'Which story are you going to let your life tell in your world? Are you choosing death with Adam or life with Christ?' Not only selfish exploitation, but also the attitude of 'going it alone' apart from God, no matter how well intentioned, ranges one inevitably on the side of Adam. Surrender to God's gift of righteousness through faith leads to life and to becoming, with Christ, an instrument of life.

DID YOU KNOW

△ Paul thought and spoke of Jesus' death and resurrection as a new creation?
△ Paul is still one of the greatest of all Christian theologians?

The New Testament in our Christian Lives

Even though it is a broad generalisation, we are aware that central to a Protestant practice of the Christian faith has been the Word of God. They attend to good proclamation of the Word of God by reading and praying with the Word as private individuals and families. We should also admit that we have not seen these practices much among Catholics. For Catholics and those forms of Anglicanism which are close to the Catholic tradition, the celebration of the Eucharist has been the focal point of the life of the believer.

Both sides of the divided Christian Church are now aware that we all need to accept everything that has been left to us. For the Catholics, this means that we are now being summoned to bring the Word of God back into the centre of our Christian lives. Listen to what the Second Vatican Council said to us:

> The Church has always venerated the divine Scriptures as she venerated the Body of the Lord, in so far as she never ceases, particularly in the sacred liturgy, to partake of the bread of life and to offer it to the faithful from the one table of the Word of God and the Body of Christ. (*The Dogmatic Constitution on Revelation* 21)

Susan Daily

For Catholics, this makes for powerful reading. The highest teaching authority in the Catholic Church (an ecumenical council) is affirming that the reading of the Word of God is not an intellectual exercise – coming to know about the past, the settings of the Church's earliest writings, the literary methods used by each author of a book in the New Testament to communicate a particular message. They are only the means to an end. To use the New Testament in daily life is 'to partake of the bread of life'. The bread of life is made available to us at a single table – the table of the Word of God and the Eucharistic meal. In the document on the liturgy from the Second Vatican Council, the Church, in a way reminiscent of what has just been said, teaches: 'The treasures of the Bible are to be opened up more lavishly so that a richer fare may be made available for the faithful at the table of God's Word' (*Constitution on the Sacred Liturgy* 51).

How can we do this? There are time-honoured practices that must become central in the life of the Christian. Priests and people must come to know the Word of God better. The Liturgy of the Word in the Mass has been structured since 1970 so that each year a cycle of readings is read (Years A, B, C) on Sundays, and another cycle on Weekdays (Years 1 and 2). Priests must be aware of

> **THE TREASURES OF THE BIBLE ARE TO BE OPENED UP MORE LAVISHLY SO THAT A RICHER FARE MAY BE MADE AVAILABLE FOR THE FAITHFUL AT THE TABLE OF GOD'S WORD.**

Susan Daily

their responsibility to follow a catechesis of the faithful based upon the Lectionary. Parish groups, or any form of group, can be formed to read and share responses to biblical texts. Many such groups exist and the practice is growing. You do not have to be an expert. Simply being together and sharing a passage, week by week, with people who share your Christian hopes, dreams and way of life can be an enriching experience.

But Catholics also need to take the New Testament in hand privately, and come to know it better. It is indeed a 'Word of life'. There are many beautiful books and commentaries to help you on your way. Finally, we need to return to a practice that has been alive in the Church since the early centuries, and lived through its golden age in the great monasteries: the practice of *Lectio Divina*. Rather than describe how this is done, I will close this book with an example you may like to use in a prayer session. From there you may be able to develop your own practices. In the end, it is a way of praying with the Word of God that makes that word your own – cutting into your very marrow, inspiring you to great faith, hope and love.

What I am recommending is not new. It was asked of us all at the Second Vatican Council (*Dogmatic Constitution on Divine Revelation* 21–26). This request was repeated in a beautiful document published by the Pontifical Biblical Commission in 1993, *The Interpretation of the Bible in the Church* (especially Chapter IV). Most recently (2008), Pope Benedict XVI summoned a Synod of Bishops with the theme 'The Word of God in the Life and Mission of the Church'. It is a passionate hope of the Catholic Church that the Word of God might be returned to its rightful place at the heart of its life and prayer. The Church originally nourished and eventually produced the Word of God. Now the Word of God lives in the Church as a testimony to all that is true. It is a measure of the life and practice of the Church that gave it birth. The Word questions the human institution of the Church when it becomes all too human, overconfident in its own *administration*, rather than forever open to the *animation* made possible by the life of the Spirit.

Let me close by recalling a hope expressed at the Second Vatican Council.

> Just as from constant attendance at the Eucharistic mystery the life of the Church draws increase, so a new impulse of spiritual life may be expected from increased veneration of the Word of God which 'stands forever' (Isaiah 40:8; see 1 Peter 1:23–25). (*The Dogmatic Constitution on Revelation* 26)

An Exercise in Lectio Divina

Jesus Christ is found at the centre of any true Christian life. The New Testament, as we have seen, is about him. It is about what it means to follow Jesus to find life in him, through belief in him. Let us now bring our journey through the New Testament to a conclusion with an exercise in prayer that asks the question, 'Who is Jesus?' The biblical text does not merely give us 'information' but inspires us to become more Christlike and thus, closer to God.

STEP 1
Create an atmosphere of recollection and prayer

You may do this in whatever way suits you, although an invocation to the Holy Spirit should always open the prayer. Symbols may help. You may like to use a candle, an icon, a picture, a religious object like a statue or a crucifix. What follows is an example of a prayer to the Spirit and a further opening prayer.

Prayer to the Spirit
O Holy Spirit, open the eyes of our hearts that we may understand and accomplish your will; illumine our eyes with your light that we might see and understand your truth.

Further opening prayer
God, the Father of Jesus, you have done so much for us in and through the gift of your Son. Guide us in our prayer, as we ponder the mystery of Jesus of Nazareth, the Christ, the Son of Man and the Son of God. Help us to understand both who he is, and to live as he lived, remembering the words of John, 'By this we may be sure that we are in him: he who says he abides in him ought to walk in the same way as he walked' (1 John 2:5). May we learn from him not to cling to our own designs and agendas. May we learn from him to empty ourselves in love, obedience and service, even unto death – that every tongue might confess that Jesus Christ is Lord, to the glory of God, the Father. Amen.

STEP 2
Read the chosen text several times

Read it slowly, read it aloud and run your eye over it so that it becomes familiar to you. Mark words and ideas in the text that strike you, or raise questions. What follows is a slightly structured reading of the text to ease the reading process.

Mark 8:27–33

Setting and Jesus' question
[27] Jesus went on with his disciples to the villages of Caesarea Philippi; and on the way he asked his disciples, 'Who do people say that I am?'

Who 'people' and the disciples think Jesus is; Jesus' response
[28] And they answered him, 'John the Baptist; and others, Elijah; and still others, one of the prophets.' [29] He asked them, 'But who do you say that I am?' Peter answered him, 'You are the Messiah.' [30] And he sternly ordered them not to tell anyone about him.

Jesus' self-revelation; Peter's response
[31] Then he began to teach them that the Son of Man must undergo great suffering, and be rejected by the elders, the chief priests, and the scribes, and be killed, and after three days rise again. [32] He said all this quite openly. And Peter took him aside and began to rebuke him.

Jesus' response
[33] But turning and looking at his disciples, he rebuked Peter and said, 'Get behind me, Satan! For you are setting your mind not on divine things but on human things.'

STEP 3
Find out something about the text

Use a commentary or a guide, or have someone in the group (if you are praying in a group) who can present what the text is about – especially its original New Testament meaning. But it does not have to be scholarly (as below). It can simply be their impression of the text. For this exercise a commentary is provided.

Setting and Jesus' question
It is often helpful to know something about the geographical settings described in the Gospels. This famous conversation takes

place at Caesarea Philippi. In the time of Jesus this village had close association with the Roman presence in Israel, along with its recognition of the Emperor (the Caesar) as divine. But prior to the Roman period it had been a centre of a cult dedicated to the Greek God, Pan. Indeed, today the Arab name for the place, Banyas, retains that connection. The setting for this crucial question concerning the person of Jesus is a place where other gods are worshipped and have long been worshipped, both Greek and Roman.

Who 'people' and the disciples think Jesus is; Jesus' response

Within that context of divinities both ancient and new, Jesus asks his disciples who people say that he is. It is not as if only Peter responds. As is often the case in the Gospels, Peter speaks in the name of all the disciples, and he describes what general opinion says. No one says that Jesus is the Messiah. They claim he is either John the Baptist come back from death, an idea that the crowds had told Herod when he asked about Jesus (see 6:14). John the Baptist is not the Messiah, but he is a figure who would come before the messianic time. Others think that Jesus is Elijah, another figure that many thought would come back to usher in the messianic time. Already in Malachi 4:5 the prophet had promised that this would happen. Finally, others think Jesus is the prophetic figure who God promised Moses would come back before the Messiah (see Deut 18:18). These are great figures, and the people who thought this way certainly spoke highly of Jesus. But they had missed the mark in the search for his true identity.

When Jesus asks the disciples, 'Who do you say that I am?' (v 29), Peter again answers in their name. He confesses, 'You are the Christ'. There is a sense in which this is correct. At the beginning of the Gospel of Mark the author announced that his book was 'good news': Jesus was the Christ (see Mark 1:1). However, there is a

sense in which an understanding of Jesus as the Christ can be partially correct, but this partial vision may even be dangerous for the follower of Jesus. There were basically two understandings of who the Christ would be at the time of Jesus. One understanding was a wonderful priest who would restore the nation to its true faith. The other was a Davidic soldier figure who would sweep away all those currently occupying the Holy Land, and restore the original Davidic kingdom. One was a priestly figure and the other a royal figure. In the time of Jesus, as the people felt the heavy hand of Rome (and remember Caesarea Philippi was a place where Roman soldiers milled around), a hope for the political restoration of Israel was strong. Indeed, some thirty to forty years after the death of Jesus the Jewish Revolt would see to the final destruction of Israel, the Holy City and its Temple (in the war of AD 66–70). Jesus must not be misunderstood in this way, and for that reason he tells them not to say anything about this (v 30). While he is the Christ, he is not the royal soldier Christ!

Jesus' self-revelation; Peter's response

Notice the solemnity with which Jesus' words to his disciples are introduced: 'Then he began to teach them that …' What follows can rightly be called Jesus' self-revelation. For the first time in the Gospel of Mark he tells his disciples who he is. He does not deny that he is the Christ, but he is a 'Son of Man' Christ. In a way that is unique and universal across all the Gospels, Jesus speaks of himself as 'the Son of Man'. He looks back to Daniel 7 where the suffering nation was addressed. Israel was under siege by the King of Syria, imposing Greek religion and practice on the nation and its people (see 1 Maccabees). In the midst of horrific threats, 'one like a Son of Man' is promised that ultimate victory will be his. Through suffering and death, God will vindicate his Holy Ones – those who remain loyal to the God of Israel. Jesus will fulfil that prophecy in his person – Messiah, yes, but a Son of Man who must first suffer, be slain and finally be raised by God in final victory and vindication. This is not the Messiah the disciples had hoped for. Peter again acts in the name of the disciples, but perhaps a little more in his own name. We know from the New Testament that he sometimes acted first and thought afterwards. He gets in front of Jesus and grabs him – he takes hold of him – and he 'rebukes' Jesus! Peter is trying to impose his will upon Jesus. This is not the place of the disciple. Jesus and his disciples are supposed to be 'on the way' to Jerusalem (see v 27), but Peter has different ideas, because Jesus is not talking about something he can recognise or accept. Peter has his own ideas, and Jesus' self-revelation does not correspond with them!

Jesus' response
Peter is in the wrong place, standing in front of Jesus, trying to hold him back from the destiny mapped out for him by God as the suffering, crucified and victorious Son of Man. But Jesus' words to Peter are not only to Peter. All the disciples run the danger of expecting Jesus to fulfil their false messianic expectations. Thus, 'turning and looking at his disciples', Jesus calls Peter 'Satan', and instructs him that he must get behind him. This was the role they accepted when they first became 'followers' of Jesus (see 1:16–20). He must go back to where he belongs. The Aramaic behind the word 'Satan' (which also provides the meaning of the demonic tempter) means 'stumbling block'. Peter is like a stone on the path over which Jesus would trip. He must not adopt that role (see Matt 16:23 where Jesus uses the Greek word *skandalon* ['stumbling block'] for Peter). Peter has fallen into thinking according to human honour and prestige. He is 'on the wrong side'. If he is to be on the 'side of God' he must adopt the place of anyone who wishes to 'walk as Jesus walked' – behind him. Disciples must not try to dictate terms in God's kingdom and to God's Messiah. A disciple, as Jesus will instruct everyone in the passage that follows, must take up the cross and follow him. To do this is to lose one's life for the sake of Jesus, and thus save it (see 8:34–38).

Susan Daily

STEP 4
Reflect on the Gospel text

Reflecting on the Gospel text easily leads us into prayer. The following questions are offered to help that process, but they are not necessary. You might be moved to prayer by the text and its explanation. Now the text belongs to you; take it wherever you wish to go with it in your mind and heart, as you turn to God and Jesus. Keep your eye on the text you are pondering. Keep it in front of you, and move between the text and your inner self at all times.

· Is this Word of God saying something to you about Jesus?
· Do you feel that this Word of God is challenging your response to what God has done for you in and through Jesus?
· As the people had their hopes, and the disciples had their hopes, do you also have hopes that Jesus would prefer you to leave unsaid (vv 27–30)?
· Does Jesus' telling you 'plainly' (v 32a) of his being a Messiah who is also the suffering Son of Man, who must suffer, die and be raised speak to your situation as a follower of Jesus, one who 'walks as Jesus walked' (v 31)?
· Can you find yourself in Peter who reacts negatively and protests loudly when the heart of Jesus' saving mission is proclaimed to you in the Word of God (v 32bc)?
· Does Jesus' description of Peter as 'Satan', the stumbling block (see also Matt 16:23) on his way towards the Cross and resurrection also apply to you sometimes (v 33)?
· Does your life call for 'conversion' because the reigning presence of God is at hand in the person and message of Jesus Christ (see Mark 1:14–15)?

Closing prayer
Close with a prayer that expresses what you would like to say to God, through his Son, our Lord, Jesus Christ. Amen.

Glossary

Antichrist – A figure often mentioned in Jewish texts, before and after the time of Jesus to name and describe a figure who would oppose the coming of the Messiah with great disasters.

Apostles (also 'the Twelve') – Twelve men chosen by Jesus to be 'sent out' (Greek: *apostellein*) on mission.

Beloved Disciple – A figure central to the Gospel of John. Loved by Jesus, he is regarded as the author of this Gospel. We are not sure of his exact identity, but he has been identified with John, the son of Zebedee since the second century.

Bible – The collection of many books that took place within Judaism and Christianity, regarded as sacred Scripture by the Jewish people (the Old Testament) and Christians (the Old and the New Testaments).

Covenant – Originally a formal and binding relationship between two human parties. The Old and New Testaments develop this notion into an unbreakable relationship between God and humankind.

Eucharist – A Greek word meaning 'thanksgiving'. It quickly became the word applied to the ongoing Christian celebration of the Lord's Supper, reading Scriptures, praying, breaking bread and sharing the bread 'in memory' of Jesus. For several Christian traditions, following a Hebrew tradition, this 'memory' makes present the crucified and risen Jesus.

Gentiles – An expression used by the Jews to speak of all who did not belong to the Jewish people.

Gnosticism – An early Christian heresy that claimed God had saved us through imparting to certain privileged and 'enlightened' people a 'knowledge' (Greek: *gnosis*) of the mysteries that lie behind the human condition, with its anxieties and hopes.

Gospel – A story of the life, teaching, death and resurrection of Jesus that attempts to communicate to its reader what God has done in and through Jesus Christ.

Law and Prophets – An expression used to speak of the whole of the Old Testament. 'Law' means Torah, and 'Prophets' applies to all the other books.

Lectionary – A book used in most Christian traditions containing the readings from the Bible chosen for the celebration of any particular day or special purpose.

Liturgy – The rituals, symbols, prayers and participation of leadership and people used to celebrate and praise God and Jesus Christ in Christian assemblies.

Mass – The Catholic and Anglo-Catholic expression used to describe the celebration of the Eucharist (the Lord's Supper).

Messiah – A figure variously expected within Judaism to restore Israel and its special place in God's design. For Christians, the expression was quickly applied to Jesus of Nazareth, but this shifted its meaning into a more spiritual idea of the restoration of the blessedness of the human condition through Jesus' death and resurrection.

Mystery religions – A cluster of religions and their cults that emerged in Greek and Roman religion. They were largely secret societies and attempted to establish direct contact with the divine, sometimes through strange and orgiastic rites.

New Testament – That section of the Bible regarded by Christians as sacred Scripture. It is 'new' in so far as it is more recent.

Old Testament – That section of the Bible regarded by Jews and Christians as sacred Scripture. It is 'old' in so far as it comes from pre-Christian Judaism, and is thus older.

Parables – Powerful stories, based on human experience, used by Jesus to communicate his message of God, his Father, the Kingdom of God, and the response required by all who wish to enter and dwell in the Kingdom.

Pharisee – A member of a sect within Judaism, beginning about 150 BC, that adhered to a strict interpretation of the Law, and the various legal traditions which had gathered around it. They were a 'people of the book', gathered in synagogues, and were not focused upon the Temple in Jerusalem.

Sadducee – A member of a sect within Judaism that was much older and more conservative than Pharisaism. The Sadducees were associated with the Jewish priesthood and based their beliefs only on the Torah. They were closely associated with the Jerusalem Temple.

Second Vatican Council – The gathering of all the Bishops of the Catholic world that took place at the Vatican from 1962-65. It adopted a more open view of the place of the Catholic Church in the world and society, asking for the reform of many Catholic practices and institutions.

Son of Man – An expression used in the Old Testament (especially in the books of Ezekiel and Daniel). It was also used in the Gospels by Jesus, in a way similar to its use in Daniel 7. He used the expression to speak of his forthcoming suffering, his ultimate vindication and his return at the end of time as judge.

Temple – The sacred building in Jerusalem, originally built by Solomon and then again by Herod, was at the centre of Jewish life and religious cultic practices. It was the place where all sacrifices were offered, where the priests officiated, and was regarded as the dwelling place of God among the people.

Theology – A discipline found within religious traditions (not only Christian) that reflects upon the mystery of God and God's dealings with humankind. Its task is to explain these mysteries in a way that is relevant to any given era.

Torah – The first five books of the Old Testament (Genesis, Exodus, Leviticus, Numbers, Deuteronomy) and regarded by all Jews as the most sacred and central books within Judaism. *Torah* is a Hebrew word meaning 'teaching' or 'instruction'. In English it is sometimes referred to as 'the Law'.

YHWH – the Hebrew language has no vowels, and the name of God is represented by these four letters in the Hebrew bible. They come from the verb 'to be' and look back to God's revelation of his name as 'I am who I am' (Exod 3:14-15). The word is never spoken out of reverence for the name of God. Thus only the letters, which cannot be pronounced, are printed.

www.ingramcontent.com/pod-product-compliance
Lightning Source LLC
Chambersburg PA
CBHW061058170426
43199CB00025B/2935